The ART of
X-MEN
THE LAST STAND
From Concept to Feature Film

Foreword by Brett Ratner

X-Men History by Peter Sanderson

Edited and Designed by
Christopher Measom & Timothy Shaner

A NEWMARKET PICTORIAL MOVIEBOOK

NEWMARKET PRESS
NEW YORK

This book is published in the United States of America.

First Edition

10 9 8 7 6 5 4 3 2 1
ISBN-13: 978-1-55704-733-5 (Paperback)
ISBN-10: 1-55704-733-2

10 9 8 7 6 5 4 3 2 1
ISBN-13: 978-1-55704-734-2 (Hardcover)
ISBN-10: 1-55704-734-2

Library of Congress Cataloging-in-Publication Data available upon request.

QUANTITY PURCHASES
Companies, professional groups, clubs, and other organizations may qualify for special
terms when ordering quantities of this title. For information or to obtain our catalog, write
Special Sales Department, Newmarket Press, 18 East 48th Street, New York, NY 10017;
call (212) 832-3575; fax (212) 832-3629; or e-mail info@newmarketpress.com.

www.newmarketpress.com

Manufactured in the United States of America.

Other Newmarket Pictorial Moviebooks include:
Tim Burton's Corpse Bride: An Invitation to the Wedding
Memoirs of a Geisha: A Portrait of the Film
Kingdom of Heaven: The Ridley Scott Film and the History Behind the Story
Ray: A Tribute to the Movie, the Music, and the Man
Vanity Fair: Bringing Thackeray's Timeless Novel to the Screen
Two Brothers: A Fable on Film and How It Was Told
Van Helsing: The Making of the Legend
Cold Mountain: The Journey from Book to Film
In America: A Portrait of the Film
The Hulk: The Illustrated Screenplay
The Art of X2: The Collector's Edition
The Art of X2: The Making of the Blockbuster Film
Chicago: From Stage to Screen—The Movie and Illustrated Lyrics
Catch Me If You Can: The Film and the Filmmakers
Frida: Bringing Frida Kahlo's Life and Art to Film
E.T. The Extra-Terrestrial: From Concept to Classic
Planet of the Apes: Re-imagined by Tim Burton
Moulin Rouge: The Splendid Book That Charts the Journey
of Baz Luhrmann's Motion Picture
The Art of The Matrix
Gladiator: The Making of the Ridley Scott Epic
Crouching Tiger, Hidden Dragon: A Portrait of the Ang Lee Film

PREVIOUS SPREAD: Storyboard panel by Collin Grant.

Contents

fore-
word

The World of X-Men
by Brett Ratner

So here it is, the illustrated story behind *X-Men: The Last Stand*. When Tom Rothman called and said he was sending me the script for the third X-Men film, I felt like all my dreams had finally come true. The words, "I want you to get on a plane and fly to New York immediately to meet with Hugh Jackman" were music to my ears. Was I finally going to be able to get a second chance to direct a comic book film? When I left the *Superman* project, I thought, "There aren't many more of these available—Raimi's got his *Spider-Man*, Singer's got his *X-Men*, and Nolan's got his *Batman*. There's not going to be any more of these iconic characters left."

On the way to meet Hugh, I started to think of the inevitable comparisons to Bryan Singer and the fact that I'd never actually made a film with superheroes in it, or anything close to this budget. The script read to me like an epic. An epic with a lot of fans. An action-packed story with huge emotion,

PREVIOUS SPREAD: Director Brett Ratner, center right, with Patrick Stewart, Halle Berry, and Kelsey Grammer (as Beast) on the X-Mansion set. OPPOSITE: Detail from a concept illustration by James Clyne. ABOVE: Brett Ratner with Patrick Stewart.

heroism, and scope, but also a story based in reality with consequences that raise issues of strong contemporary relevance. This social relevance surprised me. The concept of a "cure" for mutancy sparked a politically charged, morally challenging debate. For the first time, mutants had a choice: Do they retain their uniqueness, though it isolates and alienates them? Or do they give up their powers and become human? The opposing viewpoints of mutant leaders Charles Xavier (who preaches tolerance, nonviolence, and integration, like Martin Luther King, Jr.) and Magneto (who believes in mutant power, revolution, and independence, like Malcolm X) are put to the ultimate test, triggering the war to end all wars. The X-Men have always dealt with prejudice and persecution. But now they would have to decide: Is conformity an antidote to prejudice? Is it cowardice to give up individuality in order to fit in? Do the ends justify the means? Is great power a blessing or a curse? All of these questions resonated with me as I read what was sure to be the final chapter in the *X-Men* motion picture trilogy.

The script was so compelling, so provocative, that I decided, before even sitting down with Hugh Jackman, that I had to direct this movie. As I read on, I came

BELOW: Brett Ratner with Hugh Jackman in the Xavier School gardens.

It is an incredible journey to make a movie like this. What attracted me was not only the superhero aspect, but the humanity in these characters and the actors that I get to work with.

—Brett Ratner, Director

to realize why Tom had sent me the script. He knew I would relate to its humanity and heart. In addition to the huge, action-packed set pieces, the script had a simple story at its core: the relationship between Jean Grey and the X-Men. Jean Grey had become an uncontrollable force of nature, but somehow the love of Logan and the X-Men kept her humanity alive. The struggle for her soul was at the emotional center of this story. The many heart-felt and heartbreaking moments made the script speak to me.

Hugh Jackman proved to be so impressive and passion-ate about his character and the story behind *The Last Stand* that it made me even more excited to have the opportunity to direct an actor with true vision. Once it became official and I had com-mitted to directing the film, I went back and looked at what Bryan had done with the first two *X-Men* films. I realized that he had cre-ated what most directors only dream of: a universe with a perfect tone and brilliant casting. What I mean is that Bryan took a comic book story and brought it to vibrant life on the big screen. All his choices were grounded in reality: his approach to his characters and stories made the audience believe every moment, every cos-tume, every word of dialogue, every visual effect. It was impos-sible not to get immersed in the drama of the X-Men.

In addition to the gift of the script, I was given the opportunity to work with an amazing group of actors: Sir Ian McKellen, Patrick Stewart, Hugh Jackman, Halle Berry, Famke Janssen, James Marsden, Kelsey Grammer, Rebecca Romijn, Anna Paquin, Shawn Ashmore, Aaron Stanford, and on and on. They were Academy Award winners, Tony winners, seasoned pros. The only way I was prepared to take on the challenge of directing a cast this staggering was by relying on their opinions while staying focused on the humanity and honesty of their performances.

From the beginning, I had no desire to reinvent the *X-Men* franchise.

I simply set out to make a movie that stood on its own, yet could be watched with the other two films back-to-back seamlessly. I had done it before with *Red Dragon*, which was preceded by two very different films directed by two dif-ferent directors. With *X-Men* I had the benefit of the same director helming the first two films, guiding me toward the right tone and sensibility.

The only way I was able to take on the challenge of directing this epic was by living with the writers, Zak

> In the pages of the comic book the characters are extremely dynamic and extremely broad. But these characters are also very emotional. To the fans they are very real and heartfelt.
>
> —Kevin Feige, Producer

> It's a big thing to come on such a huge movie with a big past—one that Bryan so suc-cessfully established. What Brett has done so fantastically is to augment what was already there to bring out more emotion. He's managed to give it his own flavor.
>
> —Hugh Jackman, "Wolverine"

Penn and Simon Kinberg, who are not only very talented screenwriters but also *the* biggest fans of the X-Men comics. There is not a scene in this film that was not inspired by one of the comics, and all of these references were given to me one by one. Nothing in our story was created out of thin air. It all began with the comic books.

Of course, I must give a tremendous amount of credit to all my collaborators. My brilliant cinematographer, Dante Spinotti, has a passion and commitment that bring a level of quality and class to everything he touches. Jimmy Muro came in at a moment's notice as an additional cinematographer and A-camera operator, and his energy and creativity were invaluable. My production designer, Ed Verreaux, brought his phenomenal aesthetics, creating a realistic vision of the X-Men universe. My costume designer, Judianna Makovsky, stayed true to the X-Men uniforms, but made them far more comfortable for the actors, as well as adding her own creative touch. My editors, Mark Helfrich, Mark Goldblatt, and Julia Wong, took the million or so feet of film I shot and turned it into a movie with pace, excellent storytelling, and great performances.

I must also give a tremendous amount of credit to my

BELOW: From left to right, Patrick Stewart, Producer Lauren Shuler Donner, Director Brett Ratner, and Producer Ralph Winter.

My heart goes out to Brett. I mean—hi, what are you doing today? Nothing? You want to direct a hundred-and-fifty-million-dollar film? Oh yeah, we're shooting in, like . . . an hour. Can you get up to Vancouver?

—Chris Claremont, Marvel Comics writer

ABOVE: From left to right, Director Brett Ratner, Ian McKellen, Associate Producer David Gorder, and Aaron Stanford ("Pyro").

producers, Avi Arad, Kevin Feige, Ralph Winter, Lauren Shuler Donner, John Palermo, and David Gorder, who believed in me and supported me throughout the making of *X-Men: The Last Stand*. Lee Cleary and his entire team brought their knowledge and experience of the first two films and always provided valuable insights. I couldn't have gone through the 100+ days of shooting without Jamie Freitag, who moved up in the ranks from the assistant director of my last six films to my co-producer, and stood by my side through thin and thin, always striving for the best production value. Last but not least, I must thank Tom Rothman, Jim Gianopulos, Hutch Parker, and Alex Young, who backed my vision 100 percent and cared deeply about the end result of our film.

None of this would have been possible without the original inspiration that I found in the script for *X-Men: The Last Stand*. The actors offered support and ideas at every step of the journey. If you liked the first two movies, you will love losing yourself in the third and final chapter of the X-Men trilogy. It was an honor to be a part of the X-Men universe, and part of a motion picture that I know will continue to entertain audiences for years to come. ✕

Brett is like a twelve-year-old kid who is just excited to be on this dream project, so every day he comes to the set with this energy that's infectious and impossible to resist.

—Simon Kinberg, Co-Screenwriter

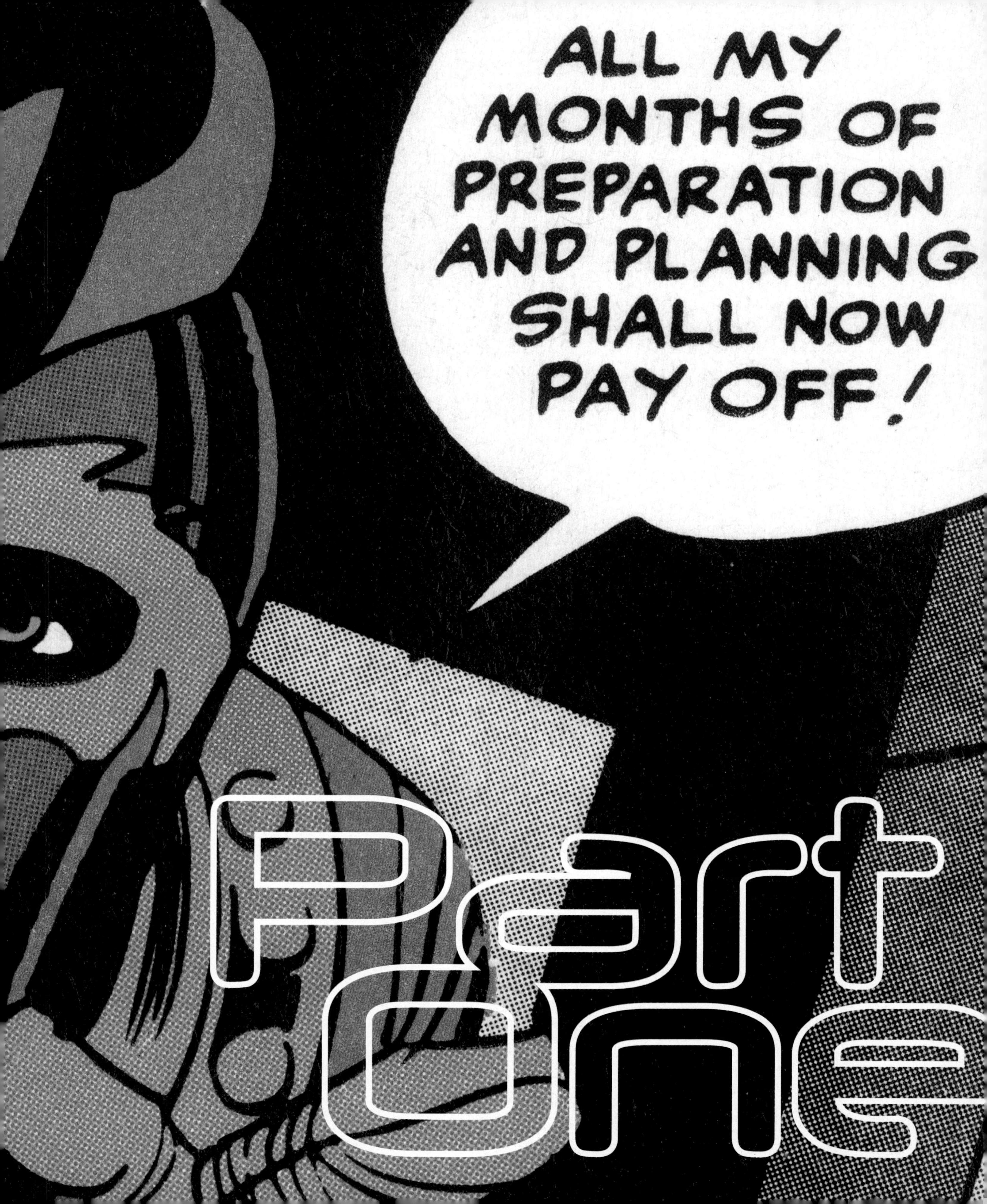

Part One

Professor Xavier

X-Men: From Comic to Screen

by Peter Sanderson

For many audience members who went to see the first X-Men movie but who didn't read comics, the X-Men were a brand-new concept. The X-Men had never become a household name, like Superman or Spider-Man. Such people might be surprised to learn that as of 2006, the X-Men have existed in comic books for forty-three years. For the last two decades, "X-Men" has consistently been one of America's top-selling comic books, outselling comics starring many characters who were then better known to the public.

PREVIOUS: The first comics panel in which Magneto appeared. From "X-Men" #1 (1963). Script: Stan Lee. Pencil art: Jack Kirby. Inks: Paul Reinman. OPPOSITE: Patrick Stewart as Professor Xavier. ABOVE: In astral forms, Xavier and Magneto debate their clashing visions for mutantkind. From "X-Men" #4 (1964). Script: Stan Lee. Art: Jack Kirby. Inks: Paul Reinman.

What is it about this series that has struck such a chord with American comics readers and now with moviegoers as well? To survey the history of the X-Men is to see how superhero comics and their audience changed over the course of three generations. It is also to watch how a superhero comic book reflects and com-

ments upon the social and political concerns of four decades:
from civil rights to feminism, from ethnic assimilation to ethnic pride, from the cold war of the 1960s to the terrorist
threats of the early twenty-first century, and more. In adapt-
ing elements of the X-Men comics to the screen, director Brett
Ratner and his associates are drawing from a long and surpris-
ingly rich strain of American popular culture.

To understand how the X-Men came to be, we must
first consider how their co-creators,
Stan Lee and Jack Kirby, revolutionized
the superhero genre at Marvel Comics only
two years before.

THE MARVEL AGE OF COMICS

In 1961, after a decade-long slump in sales, super-
hero comics were finally resurging in popularity. So
Marvel's publisher, Martin Goodman, assigned his editor,
Stan Lee, to create a new superhero team.

Stan Lee had been working in comics since 1941,
when he was a teenager. Now he was in a midlife creative crisis,
and he balked at moving back into writing juvenile fantasies
about costumed heroes. Lee's wife, Joan, suggested that instead
he write the kind of superhero stories that he himself would
want to read.

The result was "Fantastic Four," first published in
late 1961, scripted by Stan Lee and drawn by the late,
great Jack Kirby. This marked an evolutionary leap in
the history of American comics. Lee was now asking
himself what it would be like if superheroes were
real people who found themselves in the real
world. Once "Fantastic Four" proved successful, Lee and his artists created numerous
superhero series in the same mold over the
next few years, including "The Incredible
Hulk" and "The Amazing Spider-Man." These new characters
had multidimensional personalities, capable not simply of the
idealism and courage expected of children's heroes but of
anger, envy, frustration, and unrequited love. The world might
hail some of these characters as heroes, but regarded others
with suspicion and fear. Spider-Man was regarded by the public as a freak, and the Fantastic Four's Thing and the Hulk were
men who had literally become monsters.

*ABOVE: Cover of "X-Men" #1 (1963). Pencil
art: Jack Kirby. Inks: Sol Brodsky.*

THE CREATORS

Stan Lee's innovations over the course of just two years set the stage for him and Jack Kirby to create the X-Men in 1963. The late Jack Kirby not only revolutionized American comic books with his dynamic figures and compositions, but he was a brilliant and prolific source of new character and story concepts for the medium. Lee and Kirby collaborated on plots to such an extent that it is probably impossible to determine which ideas in an "X-Men" story were Lee's and which were Kirby's.

Kirby had a long history of working on comics series about "kid teams" like "Newsboy Legion" or "Boys' Ranch," and originally the X-Men were another band of teenagers. Moreover, a basic premise of the X-Men—a superhuman race (or races) divided into warring factions of good and evil, with humanity caught between them—recurs in later series that Kirby wrote himself, such as "The New Gods" and "The Eternals."

For his part, Stan Lee provided a revolutionary voice in comic book scripting: though his work can seem unsophisticated by today's standards, he could range easily from incisive humor to heartfelt drama. The best stories by Lee and Kirby merged their talents in such a way as to produce genuine, enduring classics of the comics medium.

THE COMING OF THE MUTANTS

Stan Lee's original name for the series was "The Mutants." In 1963 the United States was still in the cold war with the Soviet Union. Americans' fear of nuclear war between the two superpowers found expression in the popular culture of the period, including low-budget science fiction movies in which atomic radiation turns people or animals into freaks and monsters. Many of the superheroes Stan Lee co-created in the 1960s—the Fantastic Four, Spider-Man, Daredevil, and the Hulk—derived their powers from radiation. The X-Men also fit this pattern, since radiation was a known cause of mutation. In devising origins for two X-Men, Professor Xavier and the Beast, Lee and Kirby established that their parents had been irradiated while working in atomic laboratories.

It was felt, though, that "The Mutants" was not a dramatic enough title, so Lee renamed the series "The X-Men." In the first issue the X-Men's founder, Professor Charles Xavier, explains that the "X" refers to each mutant's "extra" power; one might assume the "X" also stands for the Professor's name.

"X" traditionally conveys a sense of mystery, as in "X rays" or "X marks the spot" or, in more recent times, television's *The X-Files* (which, come to think of it, sometimes dealt with mutants).

AN ALTERNATIVE SOCIETY

Having already presented individual superheroes who were outcasts from society, Lee and Kirby now took the concept a major step further. Each of the X-Men was a mutant, who differed from a "normal" human being through having some special power and perhaps by looking different in some way. (The Angel, for example, had wings.) Under the leadership of Charles Xavier, these young mutants banded together, making the X-Men into a society of outcasts.

But Lee and Kirby went still further. Though each X-Man had a different power, Lee and Kirby established that they all belonged to a new species, which Lee dubbed "Homo superior": separate from the main body of humanity. And it was not just the members of the X-Men who were members of this species: the X-Men's principal adversaries were also mutants. An entire new race of superhuman beings was evolving within humanity's midst.

This is the powerful metaphor that lies at the heart of the X-Men concept. The X-Men can be regarded as stand-ins for any racial minority group that believes itself to be the object of prejudice and seeks to assert its right to acceptance. Appropriately, X-Men was created at a time when the civil rights movement for African Americans dominated the news. Moreover, like most of

TOP LEFT: Warren Worthington III as the winged Angel. From "Uncanny X-Men" #132 (1980). Script: Chris Claremont. Pencil art: John Byrne. Inks: Terry Austin. LEFT: The conceptual illustration of Archangel by James Oxford for the X2 art department, headed by Guy Hendrix Dyas, for Bryan Singer. OPPOSITE: Ben Foster as Angel in X-Men: The Last Stand.

the major creative figures in superhero comics from the 1930s into the 1960s, Lee and Kirby were Jewish Americans, and perhaps, consciously or not, "X-Men" was their way of addressing the threat of anti-Semitism. (Indeed, later comics writers and the movies have brought the Auschwitz death camp into X-Men, as we shall see.)

But mutation in "X-Men" as a metaphor need not be restricted to racial matters. Any group that differs from the majority of society—in ethnic or racial terms, or those of gender or sexual orientation, or on political and cultural grounds—can see its struggle for acceptance mirrored in that of the X-Men. In "X-Men" a racially pure population of "normal" humans is evolving into a society that mixes the "normals" with mutants. This seems an apt metaphor for the continuing development of the United States into an increasingly multiracial, multicultural nation.

Furthermore, since in "X-Men" mutants are born to "normal" humans, the "normal" population fears that the mutants will ultimately outnumber and supplant them, just as Homo sapiens did to Neanderthal man. One could argue, then, that the mutants in X-Men can be seen to represent any new generation misunderstood by its elders but destined inevitably to take their place.

Moreover, whereas Spider-Man suffers on his own from self-doubt and loneliness, the X-Men find strength and moral support from banding together. In effect, Professor Xavier has gathered together individual outcasts from society into an alternative community in which mutants can interact among themselves. Again, this serves as a powerful metaphor for how the members of a minority group can interact and help one another as a subculture within the larger population.

SCHOOL DAYS

Another factor that distinguishes the X-Men from other superhero teams is that the series is centered on a school. The X-Men are students—or, in many cases nowadays, teachers—at what was originally known as Professor Xavier's School for Gifted Youngsters in New York State's Westchester County. It sounds like the name of some small private school for an elite group of students. Later, once most of the X-Men were adults, the school was renamed the Xavier Institute, making it sound like some sort of think tank for mutant studies.

In part, Lee and Kirby probably came up with the idea

of a school as a means of appealing to a young audience. Wouldn't it be cool to go to a school to learn how to become a superhero? The theme of the teacher and his young student is common in heroic adventure fantasy, whether it is Merlin training the future King Arthur or Obi-Wan Kenobi mentoring Luke Skywalker. In superhero comics the mentor theme lies behind pairing a hero with a kid sidekick. With the X-Men, Lee and Kirby came up with the first school for superheroes. This same archetype crops up elsewhere in pop culture, perhaps most notably in the Hogwarts school for budding sorcerers in J. K. Rowling's Harry Potter novels.

Inevitably, the X-Men also act as a surrogate family, with Xavier being not only the headmaster but the "father," and some of the older X-Men, like Wolverine, acting like older siblings toward the younger ones, like Kitty Pryde (or, in the movies, Rogue).

THE ORIGINAL X-MEN

The first issue of the original "X-Men" series opened with Charles Xavier, seated in his wheelchair, mentally summoning his students. Xavier, who also went by the code name Professor X, was the world's most powerful mutant telepath, able to read minds and communicate mentally with others. In his youth he had been left crippled by a vengeful enemy and was now confined to a wheelchair, but his powers enabled him to leave his physical body and travel in "astral," or spiritual, form.

On the opening page Xavier's first four students, all teenagers, race to his side. Among them is the series' young lead, Scott Summers, who goes by the code name Cyclops, after the one-eyed giants of Greek mythology. Scott does have two eyes, but in costume he wears a visor that makes it look as if he has only one, shaped like a horizontal slit. In Marvel's new comics, superpowers could be a curse as much as a blessing: Cyclops's eyes continually radiate beams of force that can stun or kill a human being. So Scott always wears his visor or, when out of costume, his glasses, which have lenses made of ruby quartz, which somehow harmlessly diffuses the beams.

Another of Xavier's first students is Bobby Drake, alias Iceman, who has the mutant power to lower tempera-

ABOVE: Xavier mentally summons his students on the first page of "X-Men" #1. Script: Stan Lee. Pencil art: Jack Kirby. Inks: Paul Reinman.

Iceman

tures around him below freezing, thereby turning the moisture in the air into ice. In the movies, frost forms on Bobby's hands, but in the comics he covers his whole body with snow, and soon thereafter with ice. Though the youngest of the first "class" of X-Men, Iceman is closer in age to Cyclops in the comics than he is in the movies, in which Bobby is still just a student while Scott is a full-fledged X-Man. (Bobby's parents, who appeared in *X2: X-Men United*, were introduced in the comics in a later story recounting Iceman's origin. Whereas in the movie the Drakes live in Boston, the comics put them on Long Island.)

Not until the third film, *X-Men: The Last Stand*, do the other two original male students finally make it to the big screen. One is Warren Worthington III, the handsome son of wealthy parents, who conceals his great secret from them: while at boarding school he sprouted feathered wings. Naturally, he became known as the Angel.

Then there's Henry ("Hank") McCoy, whose looks sharply differ from Warren's. Born with unusually large hands and feet, Hank revels in his apelike agility, which has won him the nickname the Beast. Paradoxically, the Beast has the greatest intellect of any of the X-Men, past or present, except for Xavier, and his trademark in these early stories is his copious polysyllabic vocabulary.

"X-Men" #1 takes place on the day that another teen, Jean Grey, arrives at Xavier's mansion to become his fifth student. This gives Xavier—and Lee and Kirby—the opportunity to explain to Jean (and to readers) the concepts of mutants and Xavier's school for training them to use their powers. Jean is also a mutant and has telekinetic abilities, enabling her to levitate objects mentally. Eventually she will have telepathic powers like Xavier's as well. Xavier dubs her Marvel Girl, a name she abandons in the 1970s, by which time she is an adult.

ABOVE: Xavier explains the X-Men's mission to new teenage student Jean Grey. From "X-Men" #1 (1963). Script: Stan Lee. Pencil art: Jack Kirby. Inks: Paul Reinman. OPPOSITE: Shawn Ashmore as Iceman.

COSTUME SHOW

One of the main hurdles many readers face in taking superhero comics seriously is the characters' costumes. These are a form of visual iconography that work better in drawings on the printed page than in a realistic medium like film. Lee and Kirby appear to have thought of the X-Men's original costumes as school uniforms, or even better,

gym uniforms to be worn in action. The uniforms are more
functional than flamboyant: the colors are a rather dull black
(later blue) and yellow, and baggy (except for Jean's, which
was skintight, presumably for the benefit of the young male
readers). Not until years later do the X-Men get individualized,
colorful costumes more like those of traditional superheroes.

SCOTT AND JEAN

On Jean's arrival at Xavier's mansion, Angel, Beast,
and Iceman all compete for her attentions, but Lee and Kirby
intend her for the quiet, diffident Scott. Indeed, if Xavier rep-
resents the mind and spirit of the X-Men, then the romance
between Scott and Jean has always been the series' heart (at
least until recent years, when they grew apart).

Scott and Jean fit into the standard mold for romantic
leads of Marvel series in the early 1960s, before the sexual revolution took hold of mainstream America: each was deeply in
love with the other, but was too shy and repressed to tell the
other person. Even more introverted than other Marvel leading
men, Scott feared getting too close to anyone else because of the
dangers posed by his optic beams. As a result, Lee and Kirby portrayed Scott as almost entirely devoted to his work. Xavier
rewards Scott's dedication by appointing him the team's
"deputy leader," taking over in the field or in Xavier's absence,
but Scott seems to have little real life apart from that.

Still, Scott and Jean could not keep their feelings for
each other under wraps forever, and by the end of the 1960s
they had gradually evolved into a happy couple, with Scott
even wondering aloud why it had taken them so long to admit
their feelings.

MAGNETO

In explaining the purpose of the X-Men to Jean, Xavier also asserts that it is their duty to protect "normal" humans from the "evil mutants" who would misuse their powers. On this note Lee and Kirby cut to the first appearance of the "evil mutant" who has ever since remained the X-Men's principal nemesis: Magneto.

The first X-Men movie parallels the first X-Men comic in many ways. In both, new recruits—in the movie's case, Wolverine and Rogue—arrive at and learn about Xavier's school and then join forces with the other X-Men in thwarting Magneto's new scheme. In "X-Men" #1 the X-Men upset Magneto's takeover of an American missile base. Whereas Xavier dresses as a normal man in a business suit, Magneto in the comics wears a costume that is both flamboyant and regal, complete with a helmet that seems adapted from ancient Etruscan headgear.

Traditionally, disagreements between superheroes and their enemies have been fairly simplistic: the bad guys want to steal, kill, and/or take over the world, and the good guys want to stop them. But from the very start of "X-Men," Lee and Kirby aimed at setting up a deeper conflict between the central figures of Charles Xavier and Magneto. In an early story Xavier and Magneto each projects his "astral form"—his soul—onto a higher plane, where the two debate their ideological differences. Magneto contends that the majority of the human race will continue to oppress mutants unless and until the mutants fight back and seize power for themselves. In contrast, Xavier argues that

OPPOSITE: Jean and Scott consummate their romance of many years. From "Uncanny X-Men" #132 (1980). Script: Chris Claremont. Pencil art: John Byrne. Inks: Terry Austin. ABOVE: The aptly named Toad toadies to his master, Magneto. From "X-Men" #4 (1964). Script: Stan Lee. Pencil art: Jack Kirby. Inks: Paul Reinman.

Beast

combat between mutants and other humans will only lead to bloodshed and instead seeks to make peace between the two sides. In this respect Xavier and Magneto have been compared to Martin Luther King and Malcolm X, African American leaders of the early 1960s who disagreed over tactics in combating racism. In the first X-Men movie, Magneto even quotes Malcolm X in stating he will fight oppression "by any means necessary."

Increasingly over the decades the "X-Men" comics have portrayed Charles Xavier as a visionary for his mutant race. There have been frequent references to "Xavier's dream," which the X-Men are dedicated to promoting: a vision of a world where "normal" humans and mutants coexist in peace.

THE BROTHERHOOD

In his second comic book appearance, in "X-Men" #4, Magneto is the leader of the Brotherhood of Evil Mutants, a small band of superpower mutants who aid him in his plots against the human race. Among the members of the first Brotherhood was the Toad, who, as his name suggests, could leap higher and farther than a normal human. Although the comics version of the Toad would jump at an adversary to knock him down, it took the first X-Men movie to turn him into a kickboxer.

Subsequent versions of the Brotherhood have been formed over the succeeding years by Magneto, Mystique, or the Toad. In recent years its name has been changed simply to the "Brotherhood of Mutants," since it seemed unlikely that its members regarded themselves as evil.

SIBLING RIVALRY

After Magneto, the greatest adversary that Lee and Kirby created for the X-Men was a being so powerful that he could not be physically stopped: a literal human Juggernaut. He is Xavier's half-brother Cain Marko, whose name is a fairly obvious reference to the biblical "mark of Cain." But though they are related, Marko is not a mutant like Xavier. Rather, when he was a soldier serving in Korea, Marko had found the mystical ruby of Cyttorak, which magically transformed him into the Juggernaut. Whereas the crippled Xavier's power lies in his mind, the Juggernaut is a figure of unstoppable brute force, endowed with vast superhuman strength and virtual invulnerability.

OPPOSITE: Kelsey Grammer as Dr. Henry McCoy, the Beast.

THE MUTANT DETECTOR

Early on, Lee and Kirby introduced Cerebro, an electronic device invented by Xavier that he uses to detect the presence of mutants. Although any of the X-Men can use Cerebro, it works best when utilized by someone with telepathic abilities, such as Xavier or Jean, wearing a helmet that links him or her to the system. Originally Cerebro was not particularly large: one version apparently fit into Xavier's desk—an early desktop computer. Today's version of Cerebro in the comics— dubbed Cerebra—takes up a large chamber, in imitation of the version in the movies.

PRACTICE SESSIONS

The most celebrated feature of Xavier's mansion is not Cerebro but the Danger Room, the site of the X-Men's training sessions. As depicted by Lee and Kirby beginning in the first issue, the Danger Room is the ultimate obstacle course, filled with traps and weapons, including missiles.

Over succeeding decades this high-tech gymnasium became ever more complex.

Xavier acquired alien technology that enabled the Danger Room to create solid holographic images of any menace or environment. Recently, it was even revealed that the Danger Room's computer system had become a sentient being.

RACE RELATIONS

The theme of normal humanity's prejudice toward mutants may now seem essential to the "X-Men" series, but it was barely present at first. Indeed, Lee and Kirby's "X-Men" #1 even concludes with a general congratulating the X-Men on defeating Magneto. Lee and Kirby established early on that Xavier worked in alliance with the FBI in locating young mutants to recruit to his school. The government may have regarded "evil mutants" as a threat, but it approved of Xavier and his X-Men.

The real danger to mutants in these early stories lay with ordinary citizens driven by irrational fears and hatreds of the unknown. Lee and Kirby began showing humans spontaneously erupting into mob violence, attacking

ABOVE: Mutant terrorist Rogue seeks help from her former foes, the X-Men, including Storm (far left), Colossus (center), Xavier, and Nightcrawler (right). From "Uncanny X-Men" #171 (1983). Script: Chris Claremont. Pencil art: Walter Simonson. Inks: Bob Wiacek. RIGHT: Anna Paquin as Rogue.

Rogue

NOR ANY YOU SHALL EVER BATTLE AGAIN.

individuals they thought to be mutants, including the Toad and the Beast.

The theme of racism comes fully alive in "X-Men" #14–16, in which Lee and Kirby introduce Dr. Bolivar Trask and the Sentinels. Warning of a future in which mutants will dominate the Earth, reducing "normal" humanity to slavery, Trask creates his mutant-hunting Sentinel robots to eliminate the mutant "problem." This story line set the tone for all following Marvel stories dealing with anti-mutant racism, and the Sentinels themselves have become permanent fixtures in the "X-Men" comics.

THE (TEMPORARY) END OF THE X-MEN

The "X-Men" comics have been Marvel's top sellers for over two decades, but in the 1960s they were only a second-tier title for Marvel. First Jack Kirby and then Stan Lee left "X-Men" in 1966. As editor, Lee assigned the series to Roy Thomas, the first of a new breed of comics writers who had been inspired by Lee's revolutionary 1960s work. By the decade's end, Thomas and artist Neal Adams were crafting thrilling adventures on an epic scale that made "X-Men" the equal of any other Marvel comic of its period. (It was Adams who designed Magneto's unmasked face, first shown in issue #62.) But low sales doomed the series to cancellation with issue #66 in 1970.

Some of the old stories were reissued, and the characters would turn up occasionally as guest stars in other Marvel series. One of the team members, the Beast, graduated from Xavier's school and won his own series, beginning in "Amazing Adventures" #11 in 1972. He also got a new look after drinking an experimental serum that caused him to mutate even more, growing fur all over his body. Now he looked more like an actual beast, and the new look proved popular with readers. Indeed, this is the version of the Beast that actor Kelsey Grammer was made up to resemble in *X-Men: The Last Stand.*

OPPOSITE: A gigantic Sentinel robot fires energy blasts from its eyes. From "Uncanny X-Men" #141 (1981). Script: Chris Claremont. Pencil art: John Byrne. Inks: Terry Austin. BELOW: Wolverine debuts by intervening in a fight between the Hulk and the monstrous Wendigo. From "Incredible Hulk" #181 (1974). Script: Len Wein. Pencil art: Herb Trimpe. Inks: Jack Abel.

CREATING THE "NEW" X-MEN

When Stan Lee became Marvel's publisher in 1972, Roy Thomas succeeded him as editor in chief. When it was suggested that Marvel create an international team of heroes from various countries, Thomas saw this as the concept he needed for revamping and reviving the X-Men.

The first of the "new" X-Men was Wolverine, created by writer Len Wein and designed by artist John Romita Sr. Wolverine made his debut in "Incredible Hulk" #181–182 (1974), in a story written by Wein and drawn by Herb Trimpe, as a special agent of the Canadian government who also went by the code name Weapon X. Like his namesake, Wolverine was short but ferocious. He had foot-long retractable claws that sprang from the back of his hands. Wein established that the claws contained adamantium, a virtually indestructible (and fictional) alloy of iron that Roy Thomas had invented years before for another Marvel series, "The Avengers."

The X-Men revival began in earnest in 1975 with the publication of the double-sized "Giant-Size X-Men" #1, written by Len Wein and illustrated by Dave Cockrum. Its story had the original X-Men captured on a mission to the South Seas island of Krakoa—except for Cyclops, who made it back to Xavier's mansion. Xavier then set out with Cyclops to recruit a new team of X-Men to rescue the originals. Among them was Wolverine, who clearly had had his fill of working for the Canadian military and angrily quit.

Cockrum was continually designing new characters in

his sketchbooks for possible future use. Based on some of the designs, Wein and Cockrum had created three new X-Men for Xavier to recruit: Nightcrawler, Colossus, and Storm.

Xavier found Kurt Wagner, alias Nightcrawler, just in time to save the German mutant from being burned at the stake by an angry mob. Whereas Xavier's original five students could pass for normal, attractive humans, Nightcrawler looked like a demon and had a power to match: when teleporting from one spot to another, he would disappear in a puff of smoke that smelled like brimstone.

Xavier likewise contacted Peter Rasputin, a teenager living with his family on a collective farm in the Soviet Union, and dubbed him Colossus. Rasputin could transform his body at

will into "steel" (later described as an organic substance with the properties of steel), giving him superhuman strength and making him nearly invulnerable.

Storm, known as Ororo, was the first black member of the X-Men. Xavier found her using her mutant ability to manipulate the weather to act as a goddess for a tribe on Africa's Serengeti plain. Wein and Cockrum presented her as an innocent, knowing nothing of the ways of other civilizations (indeed, she was virtually nude when Xavier met her), a romantic archetype of the woman of the world of uncorrupted nature.

Xavier and Cyclops brought these new recruits back to the school, along with several others: Banshee, Sunfire, and Thunderbird. Cyclops led the new team back to Krakoa, where they rescued the original X-Men.

It was also in this issue that Cockrum introduced the X-Men's new aircraft, based on a real-life model, the SR-71 Blackbird. This is the inspiration for the movies' X-Jet.

ENTER CHRIS CLAREMONT

"Giant-Size X-Men" #1 was followed later that year by "X-Men" #94, picking up the numbering from the original series and returning to the normal thirty-two-page count. In that issue the original members of the X-Men all left, except for Cyclops, who stayed on to lead the new team. Len Wein, who co-created the "new" X-Men, left just as abruptly. Busy writing some of Marvel's more

ABOVE : Storm turns her weather powers against Jean Grey, who has become the insane Dark Phoenix. From "Uncanny X-Men" #136 (1980). Script: Chris Claremont. Pencil art: John Byrne. Inks: Terry Austin. OPPOSITE: Halle Berry as Storm.

Storm

prestigious titles, Wein ceded the scripting of the dialogue in issues #94 and #95 to a new writer, Chris Claremont. With issue #96 Claremont would both plot and write the series. And he would remain the writer of the X-Men for the next sixteen years—an unprecedented run in superhero comics—working with a long succession of artists.

Claremont's distinctive sensibility makes him the most important creative figure in X-Men history, after Lee and Kirby. Soon after taking the writing reins, Claremont began reshaping the characters he had inherited. For example, Storm was not the African native she seemed. Claremont and Cockrum revealed her to be Ororo Munroe from Harlem, the daughter of an American father and an African princess. While the Munroe family was visiting Cairo, Egypt, Ororo's parents were killed in a terrorist bombing. The orphaned Ororo grew up on the streets of Cairo as a pickpocket, and eventually made her way to the Serengeti, where Xavier would find her.

Whereas Wein had intended Nightcrawler to be a grim character, brooding over his inhuman appearance, Claremont and Cockrum turned this former circus performer into a born showman, who took joy in his acrobatic prowess and saw himself as a latter-day swashbuckling hero and a ladies' man. Over time Claremont also developed Nightcrawler into the most religious member of the team, a staunch Catholic. Nightcrawler's religious scarification, however, is the movies' invention.

ABOVE: Following Professor Xavier's telepathic command, Cyclops fires his optic blast at Magneto's force field. From "X-Men" #1 (1963). Script: Stan Lee. Pencil art: Jack Kirby. Inks: Paul Reinman. OPPOSITE: James Marsden as Cyclops.

Cyclops

Wolverine

WOLVERINE'S EVOLUTION

It was Dave Cockrum who designed Wolverine's unmasked face, one of the most distinctive visages in superhero comics, an anomaly in a genre in which artists tend not to individualize facial features much. Wolverine's hairstyle strangely resembled the pointed mask of his costume: Was it meant to look like devil's horns?

Whereas Len Wein had envisioned Wolverine as a hot-tempered, rebellious teenager, Chris Claremont not only established Wolverine as an adult but also made it clear that the character was psychologically unstable, liable to launch into animalistic, berserk rages that could be directed even against friends.

Wolverine did not move to center stage in the series until after Claremont teamed up on X-Men with its next artist, John Byrne, in 1977. A Canadian himself, Byrne focused particular attention on Wolverine. It was during this period that Wolverine's "real" name was revealed as Logan, after a mountain in western Canada. Claremont and Byrne also had Wolverine cross a long-established moral line in superhero comics. Claremont contended that Wolverine was trained as a soldier, and that soldiers kill when necessary. His first killing took place off-panel, as Storm and Nightcrawler watched, aghast, but soon the sight of Wolverine slashing away at his opponents became a familiar one. Claremont and Byrne also gave Wolverine a sympathetic side, for example, through his romance with the shy and quiet Japanese woman named Mariko.

The last major phase in the evolution of Wolverine's personality took place in the original four-issue "Wolverine" comic book series, written by Chris Claremont and illustrated by "Daredevil" writer/artist Frank Miller (now known as the co-director of the *Sin City* movies) in 1982. Set in Japan, this series showed how Wolverine used samurai disciplines to gain control over his irrational rages. Now the man was the master of the animal within.

Over time Claremont established that Wolverine's main mutant power is his ability to heal with superhuman rapidity from virtually any injury. This power also greatly slows his aging; the 2002 "Origin" series would

ABOVE: A cross-section of Wolverine's arm, showing his claws and adamantium-laced bones. From "Marvel Comics Presents" #77 (1991). Script and art: Barry Windsor-Smith. ABOVE RIGHT: Perennial adversaries Sabretooth and Wolverine face off once more. From "Uncanny X-Men" #212 (1986). Script: Chris Claremont. Pencil art: Rick Leonardi. Inks: Dan Green. OPPOSITE: Hugh Jackman as Wolverine.

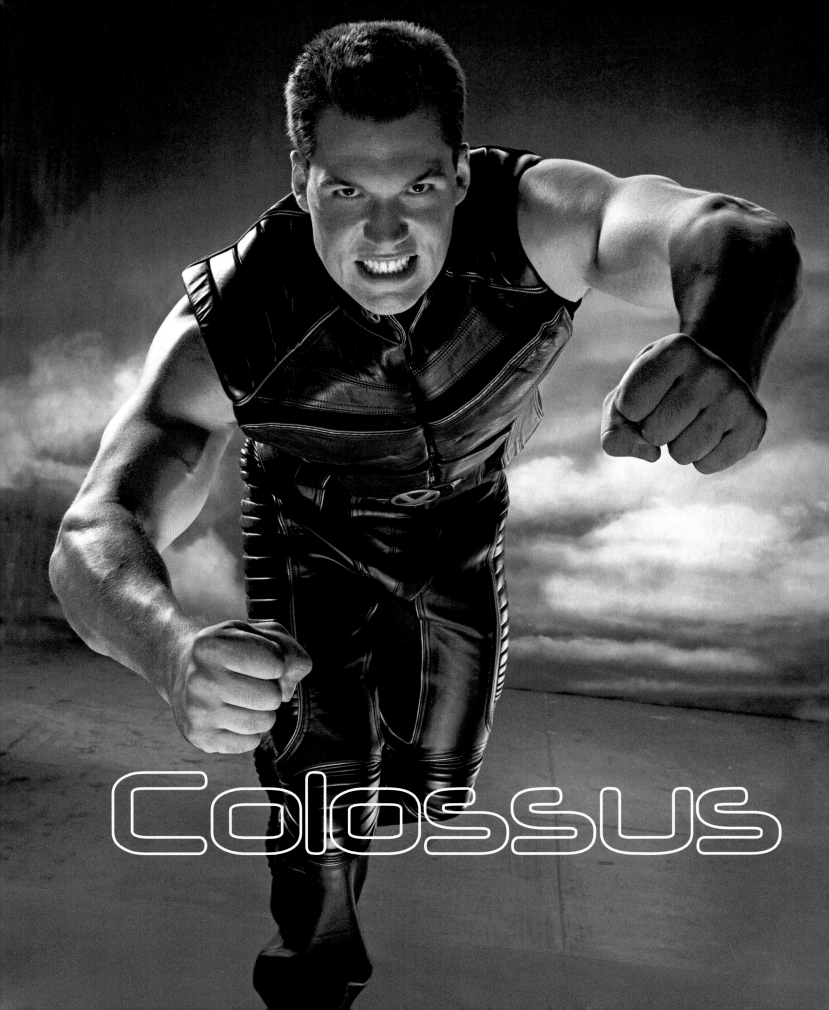

Colossus

OPPOSITE: Daniel Cudmore as Colossus. BELOW: Peter Rasputin transforms into the "organic steel" form of Colossus. From "Giant-Size X-Men" #1 (1975). Script: Len Wein. Art: Dave Cockrum.

eventually reveal that he was born in the nineteenth century. In keeping with his name, he also has superhumanly acute senses.

Claremont preferred to keep Wolverine's past a mystery, but British writer/artist Barry Windsor-Smith first pulled back the curtain in his "Weapon X" story line in the comic book "Marvel Comics Presents" #72–84 in 1991. Windsor-Smith showed how years ago, Logan was captured by the mysterious Weapon X project. Lying in a tank filled with liquid, Wolverine was subjected to a process that infused the indestructible metal adamantium into his skeleton, making it unbreakable. This image is faithfully reproduced in flashback sequences in the first two X-Men movies. The intense pain that Logan suffered drove him mad, reducing his mind to the level of a beast's, and the future Wolverine escaped to wander through the Canadian wilderness like an animal. It was later established that Logan's memories of his origin had been suppressed by the Weapon X project, accounting for his inability to remember it either in the comics or the movies. By the way, it wasn't revealed until 1993 that Wolverine's claws are a natural part of his skeleton, not artificial additions.

JEAN GREY'S NEW LOOK

Claremont and his collaborators also developed some of the Lee-Kirby X-Men characters in new directions. Claremont was very much a pioneer in writing a new kind of pop culture

heroine: the strong-willed action heroine who is the equal of any male hero (as seen nowadays in TV shows such as *Alias* and *Buffy the Vampire Slayer*).

Though Len Wein had written Jean Grey out of the book, Claremont and Cockrum quickly brought her back, creating a new persona for her. In issue #100 Jean seemingly dies while saving the X-Men. But in the next issue she rises from underwater, with greatly increased powers and a new name: Phoenix.

Claremont and Byrne's best-known story line is "The Dark Phoenix Saga," in which Jean is driven insane and becomes the nearly all-powerful "Dark Phoenix," a threat not only to the X-Men but to the world.

Watching *X2*, longtime "X-Men" comic readers perceived parallels to the saga of Phoenix: in the movie Jean's powers considerably and inexplicably increase, and she too seemingly perishes underwater in saving her friends. *X2* concludes by showing the image of a bird— a phoenix?—on the surface of the water. Jean Grey returns in *X-Men: The Last Stand*, and moviegoers can see for themselves whether the parallels to "The Dark Phoenix Saga" continue.

Claremont suggested an attraction between Jean and the X-Men's new "bad boy," Logan, especially in flashbacks to their first encounters in "Classic X-Men" #1 (1986). In Claremont's stories the rapport between Jean and Logan never seriously threatens her relationship with Scott. Recently, though, Marvel has followed the lead of the first X-Men movie by reawakening the sexual tension between Logan and Jean.

As time went on, Claremont also gave the once gentle, innocent Storm a more formidable personality, signified decidedly by the punk look that artist Paul Smith gave her in 1983, complete with Mohawk hairstyle and leather outfit. (The latter foreshadowed Ororo's casual dress in the second movie.)

XAVIER AND MAGNETO

Claremont considerably filled out the background of Charles Xavier, and in "Uncanny X-Men" #161 (1982), he and Cockrum show how, before becoming crippled, Xavier trav-

LEFT: Magneto is haunted by memories of his childhood, when he was imprisoned in the death camp at Auschwitz. From "Classic X-Men" #12 (1987). Script: Chris Claremont. Art: John Bolton.
OPPOSITE: Ellen Page as Kitty Pryde.

Kitty Pryde

eled the world, having an extended stay in Israel. There Xavier first met a former inmate of the Nazi death camps who called himself Magnus. Xavier and Magnus became the best of friends, and often found themselves debating the future of the race of mutants that both men agreed was emerging. Magnus, of course, was Magneto.

Making Xavier and Magneto former friends-turned-enemies was a brilliant stroke, carried over by the screenwriters into the X-Men movies. Magneto's "real" name, Magnus, was subsequently expanded to Erik Magnus Lehnsherr, the name he bears in the movies. (The name is still used in the comics, too, despite having been revealed as merely an alias.)

Cyclops. Storm. Nightcrawler. Wolverine. Colossus. Children of the atom, students of Charles Xavier, MUTANTS — feared and hated by the world they have sworn to protect. These are the STRANGEST heroes of all!

STAN LEE PRESENTS: THE UNCANNY X-MEN!

child of light and darkness!

CHRIS CLAREMONT · JOHN BYRNE · TERRY AUSTIN · TOM ORZECHOWSKI, letterer · JIM SALICRUP · JIM SHOOTER
WRITER · CO-PLOTTERS · PENCILER · INKER · GLYNIS WEIN, colorist · EDITOR · EDITOR-IN-CHIEF

Claremont further establishes that Magneto had been imprisoned in the Nazi death camp at Auschwitz as a child. Claremont never explicitly identifies Magneto as Jewish, and one later story refers to Magneto as a gypsy. The first X-Men movie, however, clearly depicts Magneto as Jewish in the opening flashback set in Auschwitz, and the comics have since followed suit. In making Magneto a Holocaust survivor, Claremont strengthened the character's motives. Having experienced the effects of human bigotry at its worst, Magneto was determined not to see his "new" racial minority, mutants, suffer a similar fate. (The X-Men comics also have an explicitly Jewish superhero: young Kitty Pryde.)

In the comics Magneto was once reverted to infancy, and subsequently restored to adulthood. These strange circumstances enabled Claremont to present Magneto as a man in his physical prime despite having been alive during World War II. The X-Men movies, on the other hand, understandably avoid this convoluted plot twist and simply present Magneto as a man in his sixties.

A NEW CAST OF CHARACTERS

In the course of his long run on "X-Men," Claremont and his various artists also created scores of new characters, a number of whom have turned up in the films. As

LEFT: Dark Phoenix manifests cosmic flame in the form of an enormous bird of prey. From "Uncanny X-Men" #136 (1980). Script: Chris Claremont. Pencil art: John Byrne. Inks: Terry Austin. RIGHT: Famke Janssen as Dr. Jean Grey.

Jean Grey/ Phoenix

Pyro

with Wolverine, some of them actually made their debuts in other series.

For example, Claremont and Byrne first teamed up on "Iron Fist," a series about a martial arts superhero, for which they created the mutant villain Sabretooth in issue #14 (in 1977). Sabretooth's ferocity and physical appearance reminded many readers of Wolverine, so it was no surprise that years later Claremont began pitting Sabretooth against Wolverine in "Uncanny X-Men," establishing that the two men had had a bitter rivalry extending back many years.

In issue #16 of another series he wrote, "Ms. Marvel" (1978), Claremont introduces Dr. Raven Darkholme, whom we now know as Mystique, a mysterious woman who could take the form of any other person. For a subsequent issue Dave Cockrum, who had taken over as the book's artist, first revealed Mystique's true form, with her blue-black skin. (In the comics, unlike the movies, however, Mystique always remains clothed.) After the cancellation of "Ms. Marvel," Claremont and Byrne brought the character over to "Uncanny X-Men" as the leader of a new Brotherhood of Evil Mutants. In the course of the Brotherhood's battle with the X-Men, Nightcrawler notices the physical similarities between himself and Mystique and wonders aloud whether they are connected. Two decades later it is finally revealed that Mystique is Nightcrawler's mother, a part of X-Men lore that has not been adopted by the movies.

One of the members of Mystique's Brotherhood was Pyro, a mutant who could mentally control any flame. Pyro's power was faithfully reproduced in *X2*, but whereas in the movie Pyro is one of Xavier's students, an American teenager, in the comics Pyro is an adult from Australia named St. John Allerdyce. The Pyro of the comics eventually dies from the Legacy Virus, a fatal disease primarily affecting mutants.

In their initial X-Men appearances, Mystique and Pyro try to assassinate Senator Robert Edward Kelly of Massachusetts, whom Claremont and Byrne had introduced in "Uncanny X-Men" #133 (1980). Byrne clearly drew Kelly to resemble the real-life Senator Edward Kennedy and through him Claremont and Byrne introduce into the series the theme of government persecution of mutants. Unlike the various anti-mutant fanatics who have appeared in "X-Men," Senator Kelly has always been depicted as a reasonable, unprejudiced man. Genuinely concerned about the

RIGHT: In the comics, Pyro wears a full costume and uses a flamethrower as a weapon. OPPOSITE: Aaron Stanford as Pyro.

threat posed by evil mutants, Kelly initiated the Mutant Registration Act, which legally requires mutants to identify themselves as such to the federal government. Kelly also helped found "Project: Wideawake," a secret federal project to build Sentinel robots as a potential defense against mutants.

The "new" X-Men of the late 1970s were older than the originals had been in the 1960s, and in issue #129 (1980) Byrne and Claremont introduce Katherine "Kitty" Pryde, a 13 1/2-year-old mutant who has just discovered her ability to walk through walls. (Through Kitty, Claremont and Byrne firmly establish that mutant powers usually first manifest at puberty, thereby making them analogous to emerging sexuality.) Kitty makes a cameo appearance in the first X-Men movie, leaving Xavier's office by walking through a wall, plays a larger role in the second film, and finally takes center stage in *X-Men: The Last Stand*.

LOOK! HE'S STARTING TO **GLOW** WITH THAT AURA OF ENERGY, OR WHATEVER HE CALLED IT!

GET **BACK**, BOBBY...BACK! HE'LL CRACK OPEN THE ENTIRE ICE WALL AT ANY SECOND!

Claremont had Wolverine take a fatherly interest in Kitty and later in another teenage mutant girl, Jubilee. Created by Claremont and artist Marc Silvestri in "Uncanny X-Men" #244 (1989), Jubilee could create sparks of energy that she called her "fireworks." Kitty and Jubilee both show up in the X-Men movies, but their relationship with Wolverine seems to be the inspiration for the bond Logan has with Rogue in the movies. (Yet another mutant girl, Siryn, whose voice can create powerful sonic vibrations, appears in *X2* and *X-Men: The Last Stand*; she was created by Claremont and artist Steve Leialoha in "Spider-Woman" #37.)

Another addition to the X-Men cast was Callisto, created in "Uncanny X-Men" #169 (1983) by Claremont and artist Paul Smith. She was once leader of the Morlocks, a community of mutants living in tunnels beneath Manhattan (named after the subterranean race in H. G. Wells's *The Time Machine*). Scarred and wearing an eyepatch, Callisto still looked human until her arms were recently transformed into tentacles.

ROGUE

Of all the X-Men depicted in the movies, Rogue probably differs the most from her comics counterpart. Created by Chris Claremont and artist Michael Golden, Rogue first appears not in "X-Men" but in "Avengers Annual" #8 as a villainess. She was the newest member of Mystique's Brotherhood of Evil Mutants, aiding them in battling both the

ABOVE: The Juggernaut prepares to burst out of Iceman's ice trap. From "X-Men" #12 (1965). Script: Stan Lee. Layouts: Jack Kirby. Finished art: Werner Roth (as "Jay Gavin"). OPPOSITE: Vinnie Jones as Juggernaut.

Juggernaut

Mystique

X-Men and another Marvel superhero team, the Avengers. Rogue has the mutant ability to absorb the memories and abilities of her victims by making contact between her bare skin and theirs. The longer she maintains physical contact with a victim, the longer she will retain the victim's powers. In the unusual case of Rogue's battle with Ms. Marvel, Rogue manages to steal her adversary's powers seemingly permanently, gaining superhuman strength, near invulnerability, and the ability to fly—none of which is possessed by the movie version of Rogue. (Recently, Rogue finally lost Ms. Marvel's powers in the comics.)

But Rogue is unable to control her absorption power, thus it is impossible for her to touch anyone without rendering the person unconscious. She begs Xavier for his help, and he immediately accepts her as a new X-Man. His faith in Rogue was not misplaced, and although she has never gained control over her absorption abilities, she quickly proved her worth in the X-Men, and has even served as the team's leader. But whereas in the X-Men movies Rogue's love interest is Bobby Drake, alias Iceman, in the comics Rogue has long been in love with Gambit, the Cajun X-Man from New Orleans who has yet to show up in the movies.

Over time Claremont and other writers laid out much of Rogue's backstory. In the comics Rogue's real name remains a mystery (although in the movies she is called Marie D'Ancanto). Growing up in the deep South, Rogue discovers her mutant power when she kisses her first boyfriend, inadvertently casting him into a coma. Horrified, she runs away from home, becoming a "rogue," until she is found by Mystique, who takes her in. The comics version of Rogue thus regards Mystique as her foster mother, another part of Mystique's backstory that the moviemakers have chosen not to use.

Perhaps the biggest difference between the quiet, withdrawn Rogue of the first two movies and her comics counterpart is that the comic book Rogue became a high-spirited, sassy Southern girl with a ready sense of humor.

RIGHT: The shapeshifter Raven Darkholme transforms into her Mystique identity. From "Uncanny X-Men" #141 (1981). Script: Chris Claremont. Pencil art: John Byrne. Inks: Terry Austin.
OPPOSITE: Rebecca Romijn as Mystique.

STRYKER AND YURIKO

In the 1980s Marvel began publishing complete comics stories in trade paperback formats known as graphic novels. One of the first was *X-Men: God Loves, Man Kills*, by Claremont and artist Brent Anderson in 1982. This story pitted

Xavier, the X-Men, and Magneto against an anti-mutant fanatic named William Stryker. *X2* borrowed Stryker's name for its own mutant-hating nemesis, but the movie makes Stryker a general, whereas the original version was a fundamentalist minister who sought to "purify" humanity by ridding it of the racially "impure" mutants. Reverend Stryker lacks any connection to the Weapon X project, unlike the movie Stryker.

The General Stryker of *X2* may actually have more to do with Bastion, one of the leading X-Men villains of the late 1990s. In the "Operation: Zero Tolerance" storyline, the mysterious Bastion somehow persuades the U.S. government to allow him to lead a paramilitary force in putting an end to the alleged mutant menace. Like Stryker in the movie, Bastion leads an armed invasion of Xavier's mansion and captures Xavier himself before being exposed as a Sentinel robot in human form.

Stryker's assistant in the movie, Yuriko Oyama, is a mutant who has undergone experimentation at the Weapon X Project. In the comics, she is not a mutant. She actually first appeared as a supporting character in another Marvel series, "Daredevil" (issue #197 in 1983). Yuriko was the daughter of a Japanese scientist who had experimented with adamantium—the same metal in Wolverine's skeleton—during World War II. Becoming obsessed with the idea that Wolverine had somehow stolen what she regarded as her father's discovery, Yuriko became a female samurai known as Lady Deathstrike, and fought Wolverine in another Marvel series, Alpha Flight. Then, in "Uncanny X-Men" #205 (1986), Chris Claremont and artist Barry Windsor-Smith converted her into a cyborg—part woman, part machine—with the long, sharp talons that she displays in the movie. The Weapon X Project had nothing to do with her conversion, but she has remained a formidable adversary for Wolverine ever since. The movie Yuriko is also partly based on Reverend Stryker's assistant Anne in *X-Men: God Loves, Man Kills*, and even bore the latter's name in early drafts of the screenplay.

LEFT: Weapon X Project scientists infuse the skeleton of the captive Wolverine with unbreakable adamantium. From "Marvel Comics Presents" #73 (1991). Script and art: Barry Windsor-Smith.
OPPOSITE: Wolverine vs. Yuriko Oyama, alias cyborg samurai Lady Deathstrike. From "Uncanny X-Men" #205 (1986). Script: Chris Claremont. Pencil art and inks: Barry Windsor-Smith.

WAITING IN THE WINGS

Newcomers to the X-Men may be amazed at the large cast of principals in the X-Men movies, but the films have only

Callisto

scratched the surface of the enormous roster of characters created over the years in X-Men—related comics.

The original X-Men series is now known as "Uncanny X-Men," and its sister series, simply called "X-Men," was launched in 1991. "The New Mutants" and "Generation X" each concerned new classes of teenage mutants at Xavier's school. Other teams of mutants, in some cases including former X-Men, starred in "Excalibur," "X-Factor," "X-Force," and "X-Statix." Individual members of the X-Men have starred in solo series, the most successful of these being Wolverine. For the twenty-first century, Marvel launched an alternate version of X-Men continuity, starting over from the beginning, in the series "Ultimate X-Men."

After a long, successful term writing the main X-Men titles, Chris Claremont left the X-books at the end of 1991, and has been followed on the two principal X-Men books by numerous other writers, including Scott Lobdell, Fabian Nicieza, Grant Morrison, and Mark Millar. (Claremont returned to writing some of the X-Men—related comics several years ago.)

The X-Men movies center on a relative handful of the mutants who have belonged to the team over the decades. Psylocke has a small role in the third X-Men movie, but among the many we have yet to see on the movie screen are Banshee, Bishop, Cable, Forge, Gambit, Havok, and Polaris. Likewise, the X-Men have an enormous rogues gallery, including such leading adversaries as Apocalypse and the Sentinels.

TAKING THE LAST STAND

The comics may have served as the basis for the X-Men movies, but now the films have influenced the comics. Most visibly, the X-Men have abandoned their traditional colorful costumes and now wear black uniforms, not unlike those in the first film. Scott and Jean were finally married in issue #30 of the new "X-Men" series (1994). But their marriage recently broke up in the comics, and writers such as Grant Morrison and Mark Millar have revived the sexual tension between Logan and Jean, which is a prominent element in the films. Following Senator Kelly's demise in the movie, he was killed off in the comics in 2000: having adopted a more favor-

RIGHT: The mutant Callisto's arms were transformed into tentacles in the comics. .From "Excalibur" Vol. 3 #8 (2005). Pencil art: Aaron Lopresti. Inks: Greg Adams. OPPOSITE: Dania Ramirez as Callisto.

able position toward mutants, he was shot by an anti-mutant fanatic. Xavier's school has taken in a considerably larger student body of teenage mutants—again, as in the movies.

But some new developments in the comics might surprise people who know the characters only from the movies. Most important, there is no longer anything secret about the X-Men and their Westchester mansion.

In the past the X-Men could also be seen as symbols of minority groups' efforts to assimilate into mainstream society. The original X-Men passed as normal humans when they were out of costume. These mutants were in effect hiding their true nature for fear of persecution by the rest of society. Today, minority groups seem more interested in openly taking pride in their group's identity and heritage, rather than seeking to blend into mainstream culture anonymously. And so it is that in the comics, the Xavier Institute has gone public as a school for mutants and the X-Men now publicly promote the rights of mutants.

Yet "Xavier's dream" remains far from becoming reality, as a new "X-Men" comics series has demonstrated. Joss Whedon, creator of the television series *Buffy the Vampire Slayer*, counts the "X-Men" as one of his major influences, and credits Kitty Pryde specifically as a forebear of his Buffy. In 2004 Whedon and illustrator John Cassaday began collaborating on a new "X-Men" comic series, "Astonishing X-Men." In their initial storyline they introduce Dr. Kavita Rao, who has created a "cure" for mutation, which she insists is a disease.

Dr. Rao reappears in *X-Men: The Last Stand*. What if "normal" society regarded mutation—being different from the norm—as a plague, and insisted on "curing" mutants, making them the same as anyone else? How would mutants respond to such a threat? This is the issue at the heart of *X-Men: The Last Stand*. ✕

LEFT: Korean movie poster for X2. ABOVE: The X-Men are now published around the world, including Russia. From left to right: Beast, Phoenix, Wolverine, Professor Xavier, Cyclops, White Queen. Based on cover for "New X-Men" #114 (2001). Pencil art: Frank Quitely. Inks: Tim Townsend. OPPOSITE: Ian McKellen as Magneto.

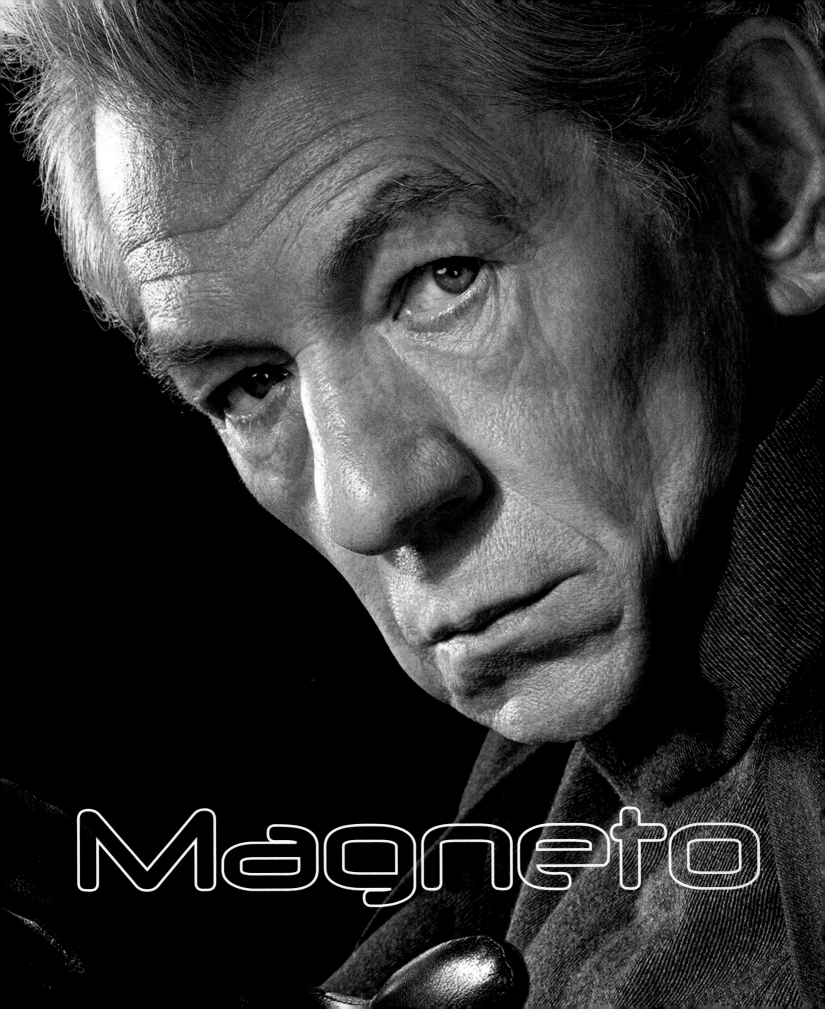

Magneto

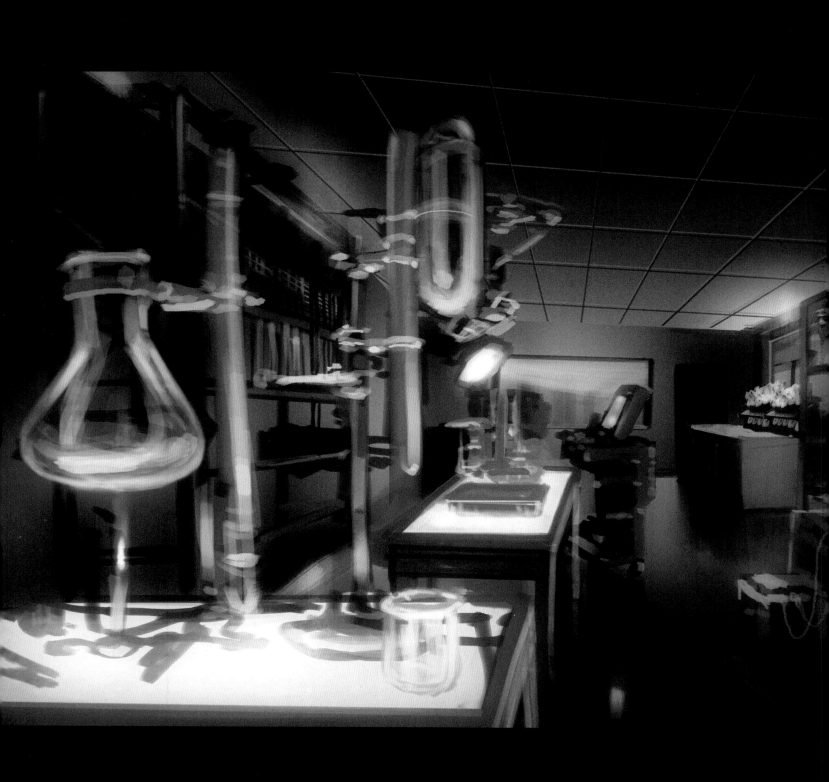

Part TWO

THE CURE

X3 - EXT. GREY HOUSE - 1985 - Prelim: 8/04/05

I am standing outside holding a hose and Jean Grey passes by with her telekinetic powers. All of a sudden, instead of the water going down it goes up. Naturally I am startled, and that is my motivation. I had a long talk with Brett Ratner, the director. He had to tell me my motivation. Now I do have a problem. This will be one of the few cameos where I have nothing to say. So I've been discussing this with Brett. This is a very suspenseful moment.

—Stan Lee, X-Men creator

PREVIOUS SPREAD: An early concept drawing for the Worthington Lab by Daren Dochterman. TOP: Concept illustration by Daren Dochterman of the Grey house in 1985. ABOVE: Director Brett Ratner (right) and X-Men creator Stan Lee, who makes a cameo appearance. LEFT: Ian McKellen (left) and Patrick Stewart on the Young Jean Grey House set. OPPOSITE: Xavier and Erik Lehnsherr witness Jean's power in two early storyboard panels by Adrien Van Viersen.

LEFT and RIGHT: Concept illustrations of Angel by James Oxford for the *X2* art department, headed by Guy Hendrix Dyas for Bryan Singer. FAR RIGHT: Angel maquette by Spectral Motion Inc. sculptor Jose Fernandez. BELOW: Front and back view of Angel by conceptual illustrator Constantine Sekeris for Spectral Motion Inc., Art Director Mike Elizalde. BELOW LEFT: The young Warren Worthington/Angel (Cayden Boyd). OPPOSITE: The grown-up Angel (Ben Foster).

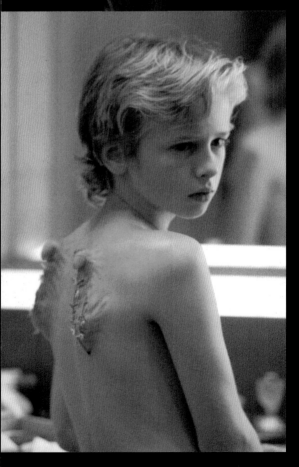

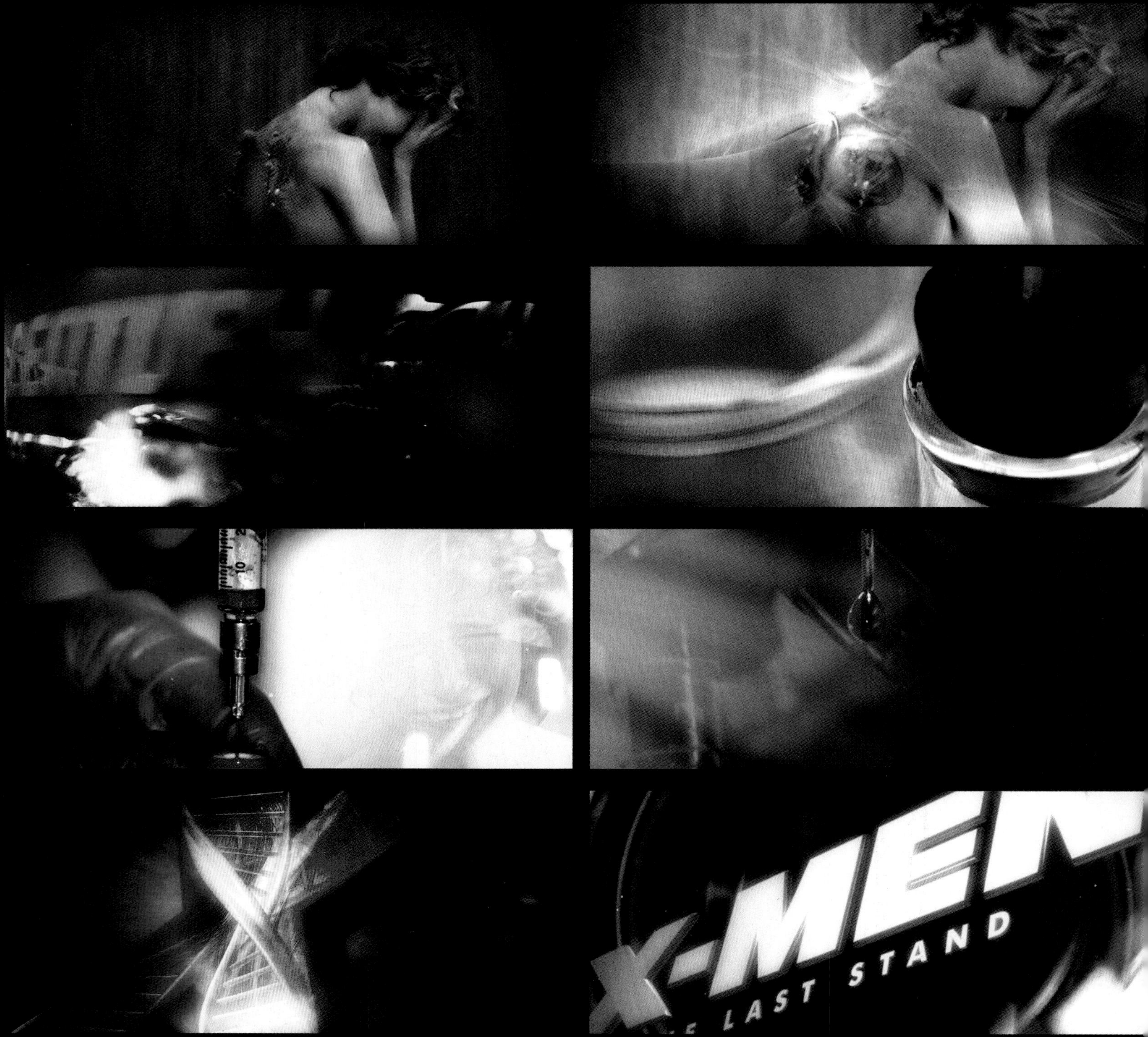
X-MEN
LAST STAND

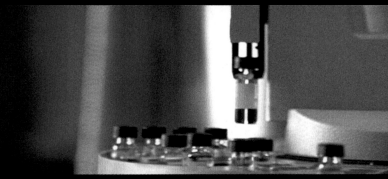

The original digital storyboards for the opening title
sequence of *X-Men: The Last Stand*, by Frameworks LA.

Storm definitely has a point of view—you
know exactly where she stands and what
she's fighting for. And she flies. She's
worn a cape for three movies and finally
she gets to fly and be part of the action.
I put my wires on, take my brave pills,
and go up there and just trust.

—Halle Berry, "Storm"

X3.069

X-Men: The Last Stand

2B

... TO LOGAN'S FACE AS HE CHOMPS THE CIGAR.

TILT UP

3

HAND HELD. WIDER. ON LOGAN.

ROGUE (O.S.): "DO YOU REALLY THINK YOU SHOULD BE DOING THAT RIGHT NOW?"

LOGAN: "DO YOU REALLY THINK YOU SHOULD BE TALKING?"

CUT

4A

ROGUE CROUCHES BEHIND A PILE OF DEBRIS ...

SHOT CONT'D

4B

METAL HAND

A METAL HAND REACHES IN, PUSHES HER DOWN ...

SHOT CONT'D

4C

PAN

JUST AS A LASER BLAST WHIZZES OVER HER. PAN TO REVEAL COLOSSUS ...

SHOT CONT'D

4D

WHIP PAN

ROGUE'S SKIN TURNS TO METAL. SHRAPNEL RICOCHETS OFF THEM. WHIP PAN OFF THEM W/ SHRAPNEL.

SHOT CONT'D

4E

SHRAPNEL

WHIP PAN

SHRAPNEL

WHIP PAN W/ SHRAPNEL AS IT HITS LOGAN ...

SHOT CONT'D

4F

PUSH IN

PUSH IN ON LOGAN AS HE TURNS TOWARD ROGUE AND COLOSSUS, ANNOYED...

SHOT CONT'D

4G

...AND HIS WOUNDS HEAL.

CUT

5

ROGUE + COLOSSUS REACT AS ROGUE'S SKIN RETURNS TO NORMAL.

CUT

PREVIOUS SPREAD: Holographic images of Sentinels break into Professor Xavier's school, inspiring a counterattack by Cyclops and the Beast (in lower left panel). From "Astonishing X-Men" #1 (2004). Story: Joss Whedon. Art: John Cassaday. ABOVE: Storyboard panels by Gabriel Hardman. OPPOSITE: Concept illustration of a Sentinel foot by James Clyne.

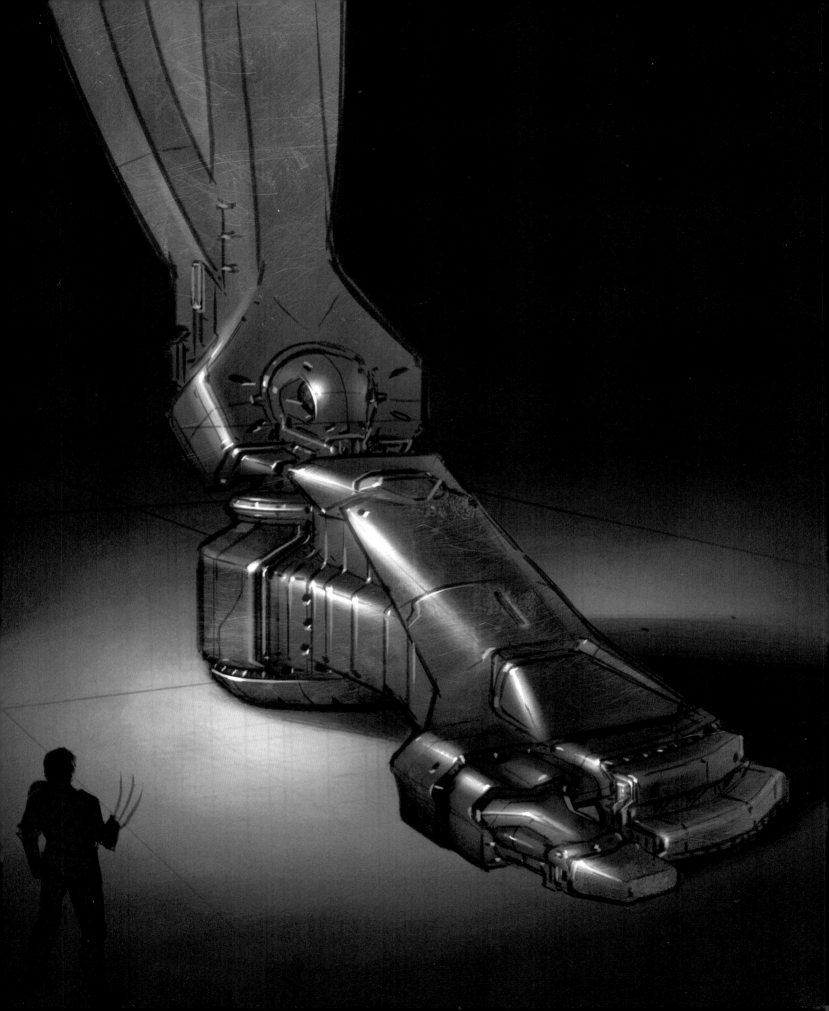

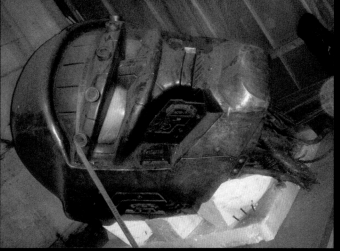

CLOCKWISE FROM ABOVE: Sentinel Battle concept illustration by Dean Sherriff; Sentinel head prop; concept illustration for Sentinel head by James Clyne; Rage against the Machine: Wolverine lashes out at a Sentinel robot. From "X-Men" #178 (cover, 2005). Art: Salvador Larroca. OPPOSITE: Storyboards by Gabriel Hardman.

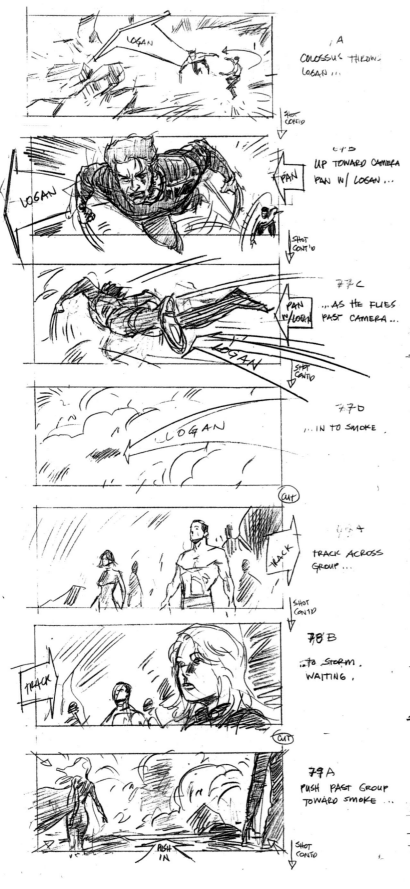

A
COLOSSUS THROWS
LOGAN ...

67 D
UP TOWARD CAMERA
PAN W/ LOGAN ...

77 C
... AS HE FLIES
PAST CAMERA ...

77 D
... IN TO SMOKE.

CUT

78 A
TRACK ACROSS
GROUP ...

78 B
... TO STORM.
WAITING.

CUT

79 A
PUSH PAST GROUP
TOWARD SMOKE ...

PUSH IN

79 B
... AS SOMETHING
FLIES TO CAMERA ...

SMASH IN

79 C
IT HITS GROUND .W/
LOGAN ATTACHED ...

79 D
SENTINAL HEAD
COMES TO REST
IN F.G.

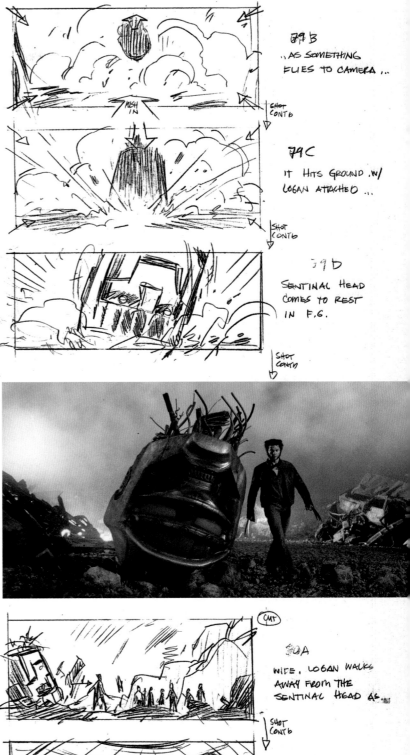

CUT

80 A
WIFE. LOGAN WALKS
AWAY FROM THE
SENTINAL HEAD AS ...

80 B
THE WORLD DISSOLVES
REVEALING THE
DANGER ROOM.

CUT

DANGER ROOM CONCEPT
4 NOV 2005

We don't see a whole lot of the actual
Danger Room itself. What we see is a
Danger Room that's more a large
multi-media game room that is capable
of projecting you into various environ-
ments. At first we don't even know
that we're in the Danger Room.

—Ed Verreaux, Production Designer

ABOVE LEFT, RIGHT, and BELOW RIGHT: Danger
Room concepts showing its holographic nature
by Assistant Art Director Andrew Li. BELOW LEFT:
Danger Room concept illustration by Assistant
Art Director Paolo Venturi.

DAN
10 NOV

DANGER ROOM CONCEPT
4 NOV 2005

M CONCEPT

X3.075

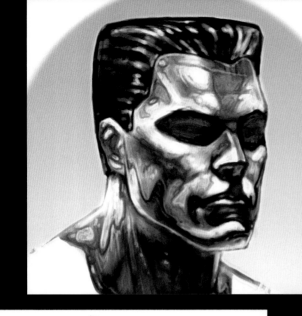

Colossus is a younger mutant—the strong and silent type—whose skin turns to organic metal and who gains superhuman strength. I'm exactly the same size as Colossus in the comic book, six foot seven, two hundred and fifty-five pounds. But when the character actually mutates he grows to seven feet, five hundred pounds. I can't quite compete with that. That's where the guys in CGI help out.

—Daniel Cudmore, "Colossus"

OPPOSITE: In "organic steel" form, Colossus demonstrates his superhuman strength by uprooting a tree stump. From "Uncanny X-Men" #140 (1980). Script: Chris Claremont. Pencil art: John Byrne. Inks: Terry Austin. LEFT and TOP LEFT: Conceptual illustrations of Colossus' body armor by Constantine Sekeris for Spectral Motion Inc. ABOVE CENTER and RIGHT: Face masks worn by actor Daniel Cudmore created by Spectral Motion Inc. The masks are molded from Daniel Cudmore's face and worn by the actor for visual and digital effects enhancement reference. RIGHT: Actor Daniel Cudmore.

X3.077

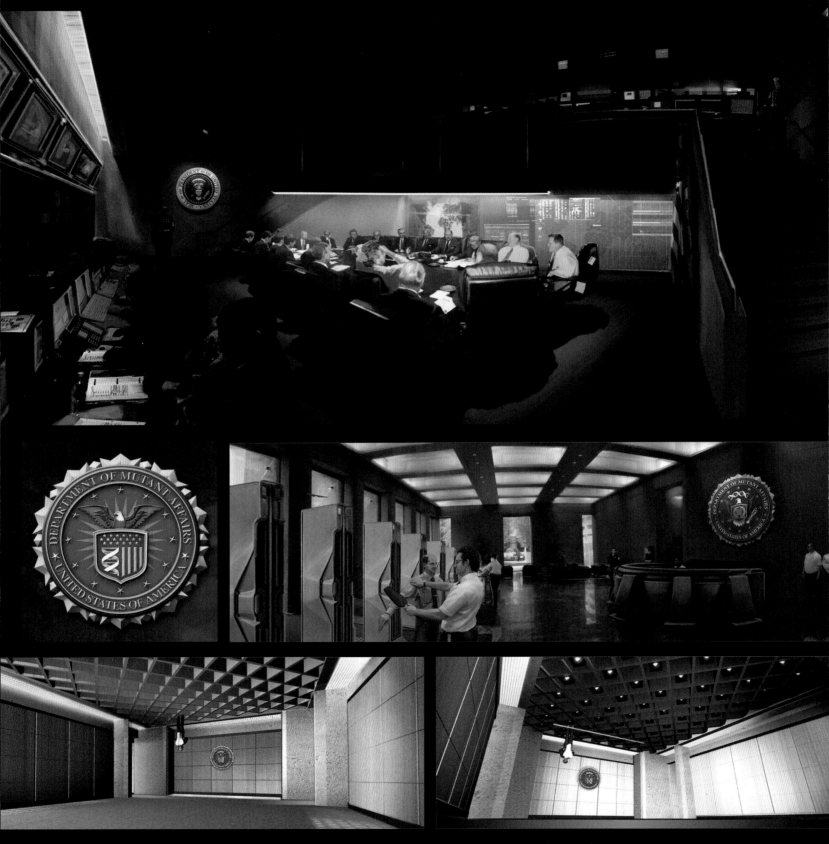

078.X3

When I originally wrote Beast, I wanted him to go against type. Even though he looked the most animalistic and savage, he was the most erudite, the most learned, he always used big words almost as if he were a professor of literature.

—Stan Lee

OPPOSITE TOP: Concept drawing by Jeff Julian of the President's secret meeting room. OPPOSITE MIDDLE LEFT: Department of Mutant Affairs crest designed by Ray Lai. OPPOSITE MIDDLE RIGHT: Concept drawing of the Department of Mutant Affairs lobby by Jeff Julian. OPPOSITE BELOW: Computer-generated set renderings of Hank McCoy's office by Paolo Venturi. ABOVE: Josef Sommer as the U.S. President and Kelsey Grammer as Hank McCoy (a k a Beast). LEFT: The crew sets up the opening scene in Hank McCoy's office, created from the facing illustrations.

Beast always fell to the wayside because it's an expensive character in terms of makeup and prosthetics. You also want to have a large role to justify putting an actor through that process. We were lucky enough to get Kelsey Grammer. You can't see Kelsey through the makeup, but you hear his wonderful voice and he nails all of the comic book tics perfectly.

—David Gorder, Associate Producer

ABOVE: Illustrations of Beast with curly hair, fangs, and glasses by Constantine Sekeris for Spectral Motion Inc. All other illustrations by Carlos Huante for Spectral Motion Inc.
BELOW: Special Effects Make-Up Artists Bart Mixon, left, and Thom Floutz touch up Kelsey Grammer on set.

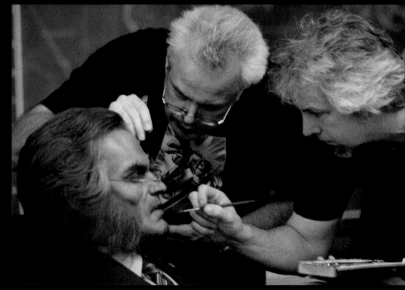

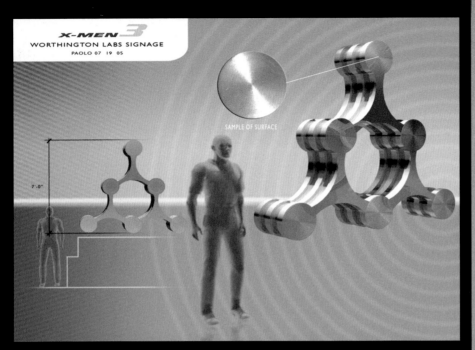

X-MEN 3
WORTHINGTON LABS SIGNAGE
PAOLO 07 19 05

SAMPLE OF SURFACE

7'-0"

ABOVE and BELOW: The Worthington Labs corporate logo designed by Paolo Venturi showing scale and texture, and a photo composition by Andrew Campbell integrating the logo into the set. OPPOSITE: Dr. Kavita Rao (Shohreh Aghdashloo) and Warren Worthington II (Michael Murphy) look out the window of Worthington Labs.

WORTHINGTON LABS

X3.083

ABOVE and LEFT: Concept drawings of Worthington Labs by Daren Dochterman. BELOW: Leech/Jimmy (Cameron Bright) peers from the window of his containment room at the Worthington Labs Alcatraz facility. OPPOSITE ABOVE: Beast visiting Leech in his room. OPPOSITE BELOW LEFT: Concept illustration for Leech's room by Daren Dochterman. OPPOSITE BELOW RIGHT: Photo of Leech's/Jimmy's room at Alcatraz Island by the on-set dresser Pat Kearns. The set was known as The White Room.

The inner sanctum of the laboratory is a special room that the character Leech is living in. It is the cleanest room—it's just a white room. Then you step outside and it's not quite so white. Step a little bit further out and there are these still very clean high-tech corridors. It gives a sense of layers within layers within layers.

—Ed Verreaux,
Production Designer

The "cure" is a way to distill or diminish everyone into the same person. And I don't think you want to do that.

—Kelsey Grammer, "Beast"

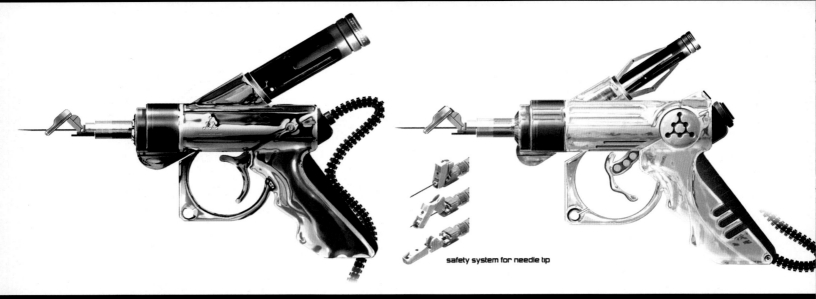

safety system for needle tip

serum vile is inserted here and is held in place by a 'claw' extruding from the guns syringe area

ABOVE: Concept illustrations for the "cure" serum administering device by Concept Illustrator Warren Flanagan. OPPOSITE LEFT: More administering device concepts by Ron Turner. OPPOSITE: serum vials by Warren Flanagan. BELOW: Concepts for serum and serum vials by Warren Flanagan. RIGHT: Dr. Rao prepares serum for use on Warren Worthington III/ Angel played by Ben Foster.

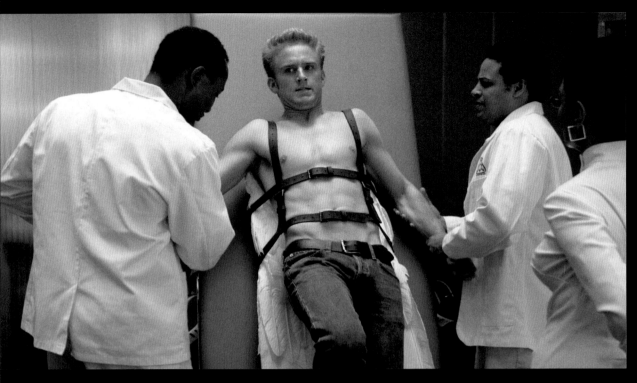

Angel wings may be considered beautiful
but they certainly make you stick out.
—Ben Foster, "Angel"

X3.089

OPPOSITE: Cyclops (James Marsden) on his custom-built X-Men Harley-Davidson. CLOCKWISE FROM ABOVE: Early concept illustration of the Phoenix rising effect at Alkali Lake by Paolo Venturi; storyboards by Brent Boates; Phoenix rising illustration by Paolo Venturi; and Cyclops (James Marsden) responding to "voices" on the shores of Alkali Lake.

AL-1 We see the surface of the lake swell...the light rising below...

AL-2 ...light shards... water defies gravity...

AL-3 Dark Pheonix rises above the lake..

ABOVE and OPPOSITE: Concept illustrations of Phoenix rising out of Alkali Lake by James Clyne. LEFT: Phoenix illustration from the Marvel archives by Julie Bell, 1996. BELOW LEFT: Visual effect stills of Jean Grey rising out of Alkali Lake. BELOW: Storyboard panels by Rick Newsome.

STAR DESCENDS, MAELSTROM OF GRAVITY...

092.X3

ABOVE: Phoenix Rising: Jean Grey first appears from the waters in her more powerful incarnation of Phoenix. From "X-Men" #101 (1976). Script: Chris Claremont. Pencil art: Dave Cockrum. Inks: Frank Chiaramonte. RIGHT: The resurrected Jean Grey confronts Scott/Cyclops.

ABOVE: Cyclops and Jean Grey share a final moment. LEFT: Wolverine searches for Scott and finds an ominous sign. RIGHT: Wolverine and Storm find the comatose Jean Grey.

ABOVE: An illustration highlighting the X-Jet weapons by Jeff Julian. BELOW LEFT and RIGHT: Early concept drawings of the X-Jet by James Clyne. OPPOSITE ABOVE: The X-Jet in its underground hangar at the X-Mansion by Sean Goojha. The set would be completely computer-generated. OPPOSITE BELOW: Illustration of the X-Jet landing at Alkali Lake by James Clyne.

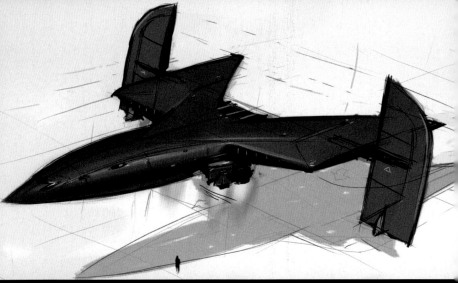

X-JET COCKPIT WITH NEW CONSOLES
20 JUL 2005

OPPOSITE: Kitty Pryde/Shadowcat (Ellen Page) is buck-
led in for takeoff. ABOVE: Interior illustrations of the
X-Jet by Jeff Julian. LEFT: Concept illustrations by
Andrew Li of the larger, redesigned X-Jet cockpit with
new consoles. BELOW: Rear view concept illustrations
of the X-Jet interior by Andrew Li.

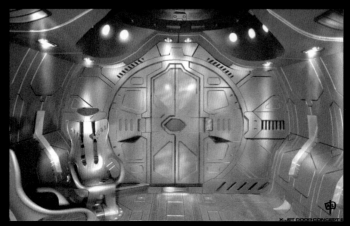

Most of the established characters we left the same in feeling, while other characters we decided to completely update. Storm got a more modern haircut and a lot of black and more-fitted clothes.

For Dark Phoenix we didn't want to go as far as the comics where she's in a cat suit, but she had to be sexy. We shot outside and it was cold, so she also needed a coat. According to Marvel, Dark Phoenix can wear green or red, and since Rogue always wears green, we went with red.

We wanted Angel to be a New York Upper East Side rich boy with a preppy—but still cool—look. What made his costumes particularly challenging was that we needed three versions of everything. One version was made to accommodate prosthetic wings, another version was made so his clothes looked natural over the wings, and the third set was just normal clothes used when the wings are CG.

Beast works in Washington and mostly wears suits, so building suits that looked natural on his prosthetic body was the challenge. For his X-Suit we had this idea that it was really old, that he drags it out of mothballs, so it's slightly cracked and looks very seventies; a little too tight and too small. Kelsey was a good sport about it.

—Judianna Makovsky, Costume Designer

Costume designer Judianna Makovsky's ideas for Dark Phoenix (shown on Famke Janssen, left), Storm's flight suit (both sketches by Susan Zarate), and Beast's retired X-Men uniform (sketch by Robert Miller). Halle Berry, as Storm, wears a lace blouse designed by Judianna Makovsky.

Part Three

THE BROTHERHOOD

PREVIOUS SPREAD: Concept illustration by James Clyne of the mutant meeting—a gathering of mutants opposed to the cure. ABOVE: Street posters advertising the mutant meeting. LEFT: Paolo Venturi's concept drawing of the dilapidated church set for the meeting. BELOW: Interior of the church by Warren Flanagan. OPPOSITE TOP: Magneto (Ian McKellen) leads the meeting. OPPOSITE BELOW LEFT: Callisto (Dania Ramirez) wearing variations of the "Omega Mutie" tattoo. OPPOSITE BELOW RIGHT: Digitally created Phat attends the meeting. OPPOSITE INSET: The Omega Mutie tattoo, designed by Ray Lai, marks those who are on Magneto's side.

You have to decide what you're going to do about your difference. Are you going to fit in? Are you going to try to be like everybody else? Or are you going to point out your difference and be proud of it?

—Ian McKellen, "Magneto"

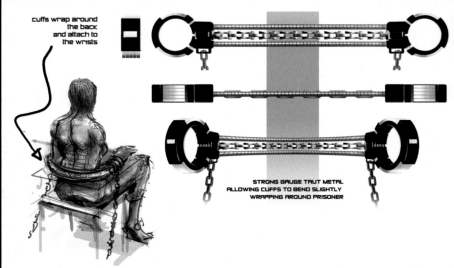

cuffs wrap around
the back
and attach to
the wrists

STRONG GAUGE TRAUT METAL
ALLOWING CUFFS TO BEND SLIGHTLY
WRAPPING AROUND PRISONER

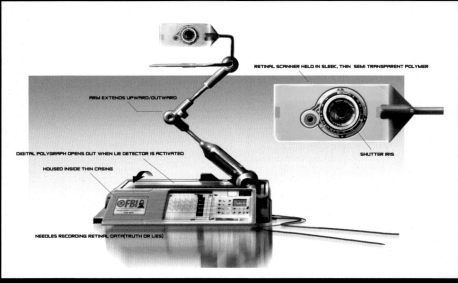

RETINAL SCANNER HELD IN SLEEK, THIN SEMI TRANSPARENT POLYMER

ARM EXTENDS UPWARD/OUTWARD

DIGITAL POLYGRAPH OPENS OUT WHEN LIE DETECTOR IS ACTIVATED

SHUTTER IRIS

HOUSED INSIDE THIN CASING

FBI

NEEDLES RECORDING RETINAL DATA (TRUTH OR LIES)

OPPOSITE LEFT and RIGHT: Illustrations of Mystique by Spectral Motion Inc. illustrator Tashiro Kiya. OPPOSITE RIGHT TOP: Designs for Mystique's handcuffs by Warren Flanagan. OPPOSITE RIGHT MIDDLE: Concept for interrogation retinal scanner by Warren Flanagan and Milena Zdravkovic. BELOW: Warren Flanagan's concept drawing of Mystique's interrogation. ABOVE: Five of the forty-plus team of *X3* makeup artists were needed to apply Mystique's unique look—a process that typically took 5 hours.

LEFT: Concept drawing of the Blue Infirmary in the X-Mansion by Christopher Ross. Stills: Xavier (Patrick Stewart) tries to control Jean Grey's (Famke Janssen) mounting power. Wolverine speaks to Jean and witnesses her power firsthand. OPPOSITE BOTTOM LEFT: Concept illustration of the headsensor helmet by Warren Flanagan.

FRONT VISOR IS TRANSPARENT AND GRADUALLY RECEDES TO A FROSTED MATERIAL.

SENSORS ACTIVATE/PULSE ONCE THE HEADSET IS IN PLACE.

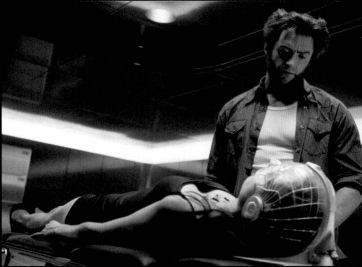

Well, unrequited love is more
interesting than requited love.

—Stan Lee

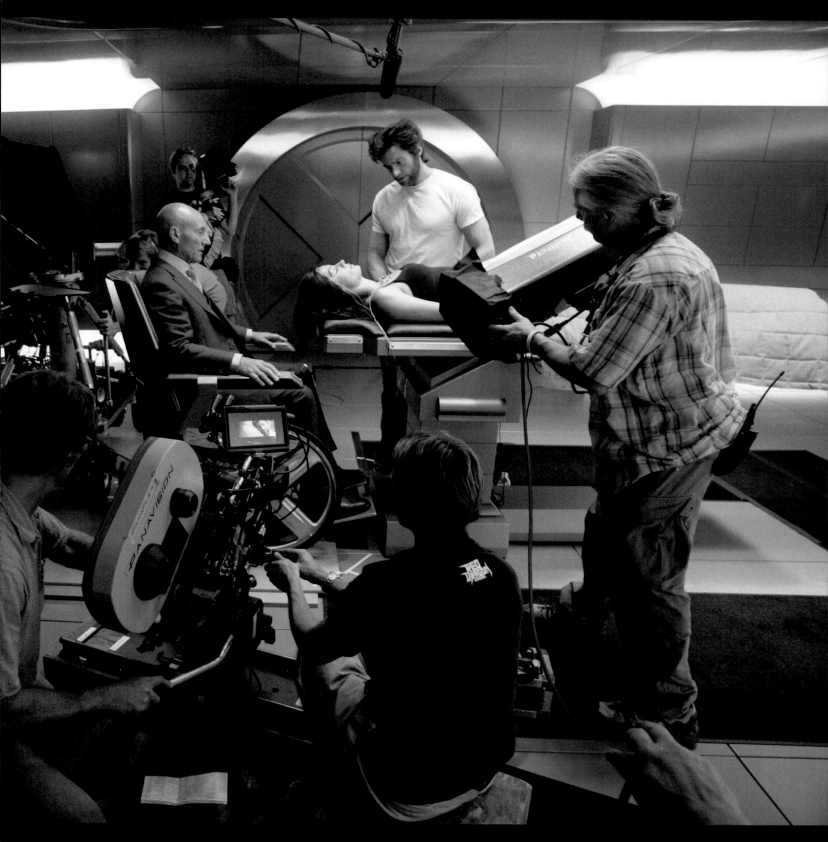

Kitty is homesick and Iceman—he's a sweetheart—he's trying to make her feel better, so he says "Come with me," and he turns the fountain into an ice rink. There is this very interesting special effects scene. It's magic, but touching. It's all within a story, so the effect, as magical as it is, is there to enhance the story and create a feel within the movie.

—Avi Arad, Producer

OPPOSITE: Concepts for the frozen fountain by Warren Flanagan. OPPOSITE BELOW: Frozen "ice" skates by Warren Flanagan. BELOW: concept for frozen fountain by Paolo Venturi.

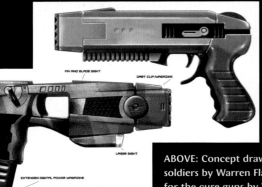

ABOVE: Concept drawings for anti-mutant soldiers by Warren Flanagan. LEFT: Concepts for the cure guns by Warren Flanagan. BELOW: Concept drawing of Pyro's attack on the cure clinic by Warren Flanagan. RIGHT: Paolo Venturi's concept for a cure clinic.

ABOVE: Paolo Venturi's illustration of the cure clinic. RIGHT: Concept illustrations of the anti-mutant soldier guns by Warren Flanagan. BELOW: Early concept illustration of an anti-mutant soldier by Daren Dochterman.

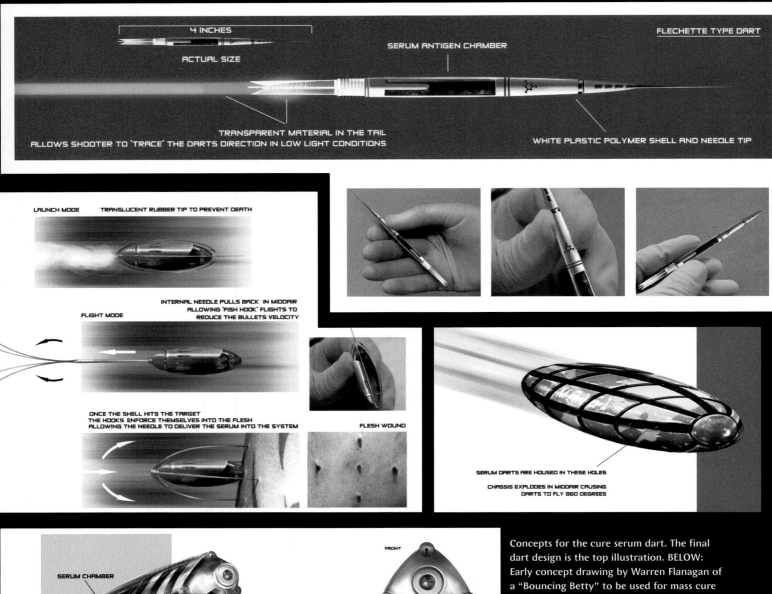

4 INCHES

ACTUAL SIZE

FLECHETTE TYPE DART

SERUM ANTIGEN CHAMBER

TRANSPARENT MATERIAL IN THE TAIL
ALLOWS SHOOTER TO 'TRACE' THE DARTS DIRECTION IN LOW LIGHT CONDITIONS

WHITE PLASTIC POLYMER SHELL AND NEEDLE TIP

LAUNCH MODE   TRANSLUCENT RUBBER TIP TO PREVENT DEATH

FLIGHT MODE

INTERNAL NEEDLE PULLS BACK IN MIDDAIR
ALLOWING 'FISH HOOK' FLIGHTS TO
REDUCE THE BULLETS VELOCITY

ONCE THE SHELL HITS THE TARGET
THE HOOKS ENFORCE THEMSELVES INTO THE FLESH
ALLOWING THE NEEDLE TO DELIVER THE SERUM INTO THE SYSTEM

FLESH WOUND

SERUM DARTS ARE HOUSED IN THESE HOLES

CHASSIS EXPLODES IN MIDDAIR CAUSING
DARTS TO FLY 360 DEGREES

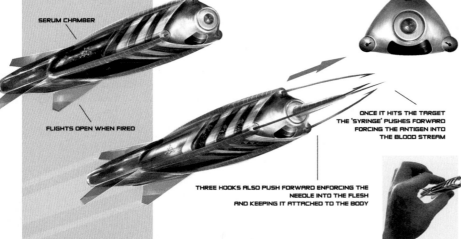

SERUM CHAMBER

FRONT

FLIGHTS OPEN WHEN FIRED

ONCE IT HITS THE TARGET
THE 'SYRINGE' PUSHES FORWARD
FORCING THE ANTIGEN INTO
THE BLOOD STREAM

THREE HOOKS ALSO PUSH FORWARD ENFORCING THE
NEEDLE INTO THE FLESH
AND KEEPING IT ATTACHED TO THE BODY

Concepts for the cure serum dart. The final
dart design is the top illustration. BELOW:
Early concept drawing by Warren Flanagan of
a "Bouncing Betty" to be used for mass cure
dart dispersal.

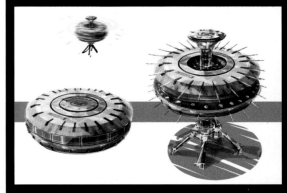

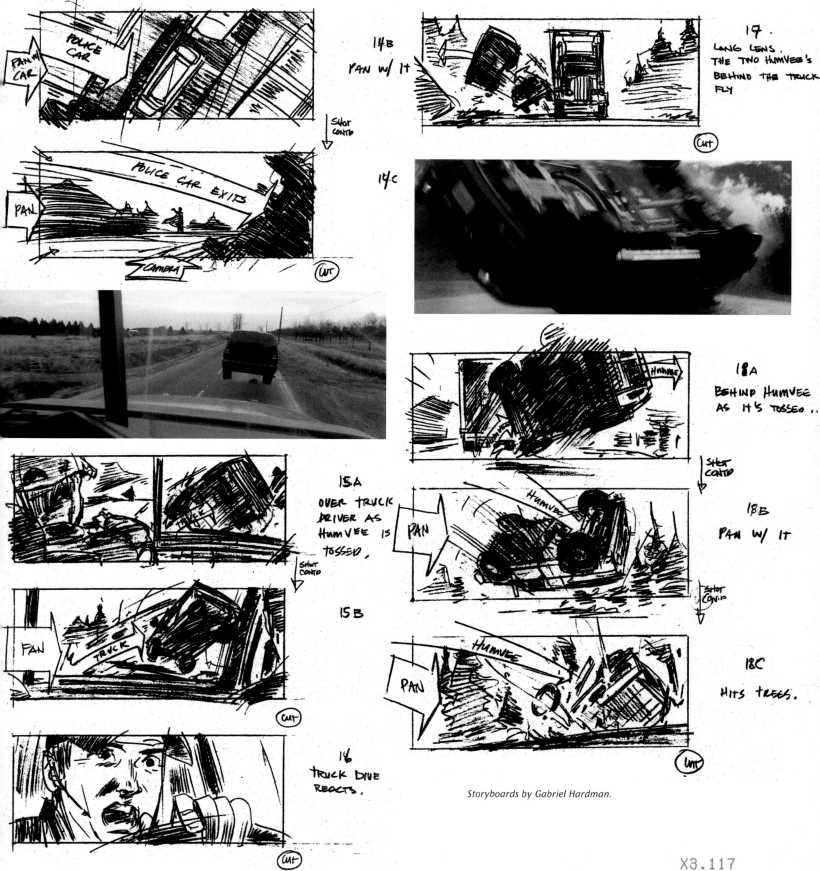

14B
PAN W/ IT

SHOT
CONTD

14C

17.
LONG LENS.
THE TWO HUMVEE'S
BEHIND THE TRUCK
FLY

CUT

18A
BEHIND HUMVEE
AS IT'S TOSSED...

SHOT
CONTD

15A
OVER TRUCK
DRIVER AS
HUMVEE IS
TOSSED.

SHOT
CONTD

18B
PAN W/ IT

SHOT
CONTD

15B

CUT

18C
HITS TREES.

16
TRUCK DRIVE
REACTS.

CUT

Storyboards by Gabriel Hardman.

CUT

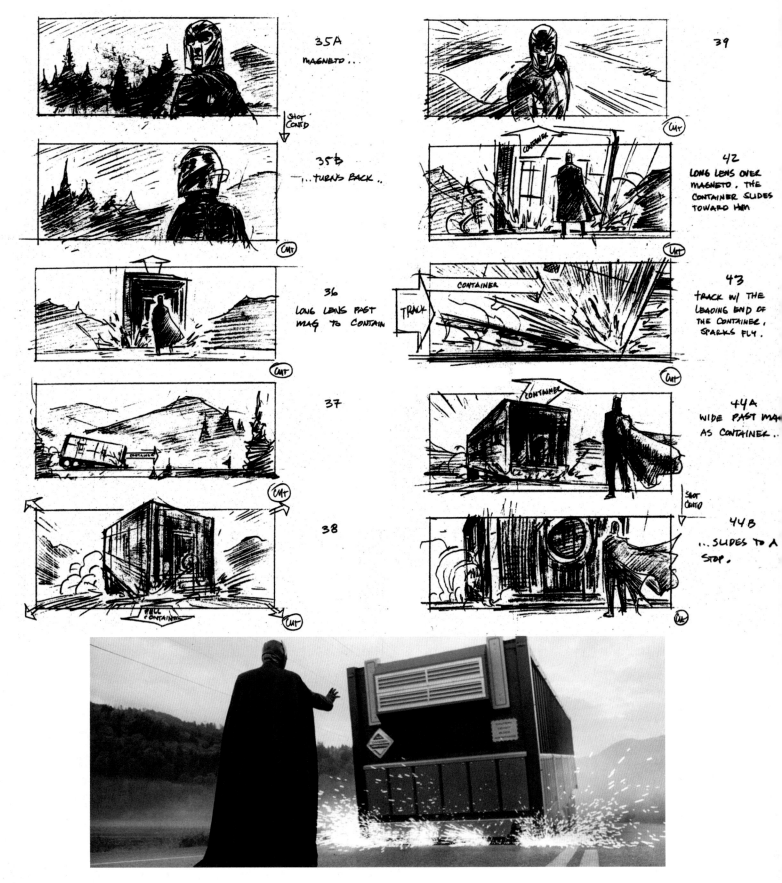

35A
MAGNETO..

SHOT CONT'D

35B
...TURNS BACK..

36
LONG LENS PAST
MAG TO CONTAIN

37

38
ROLL CONTAINER

39

42
LONG LENS OVER
MAGNETO. THE
CONTAINER SLIDES
TOWARD HIM

43
TRACK W/ THE
LEADING END OF
THE CONTAINER.
SPARKS FLY.

44A
WIDE PAST MAG
AS CONTAINER..

SHOT CONT'D

44B
...SLIDES TO A
STOP.

118.X3

Storyboards by Gabriel Hardman.

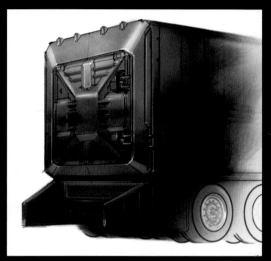

X-MEN 3
INT. PRISON TRAILER CONVOY
SEP 2005

ABOVE LEFT: Concept illustrations of the interior of the prison truck by Paolo Venturi/Andrew Li. ABOVE RIGHT: Back of truck concept drawings by James Clyne. BELOW RIGHT: *X-Men: The Last Stand* film editors—from left to right, Mark Helfrich, Julia Wong, and Mark Goldblatt—on the set in Vancouver. BELOW: Concept drawing of the truck exterior by Paolo Venturi.

One enjoyable aspect about X-Men is that neither the word *villain* nor *hero* is quite right. It's a bit more sophisticated than that. There is good and ill behavior in each of us.

—Ian McKellen

ABOVE: Concept drawing of Mystique's prison cell on the convoy truck by Daren Dochterman.

JUGGERNAUT RESTRAINT SYSTEM

For Juggernaut the prosthetic people were building the body and we
really couldn't do anything until his
body arrived. Concept artists gave
us drawings and we created costumes from the drawings. On a
film like this the prosthetics, the
makeup and hair, and costume
work in tandem.

— Judianna Makovsky, Costume Designer

OPPOSITE AND ABOVE: Dean Sherriff's concept illustra-
tions for Juggernaut's restraints on the convoy truck.
BELOW: More Juggernaut restraint concepts by
Constantine Sekeris for Spectral Motion Inc.

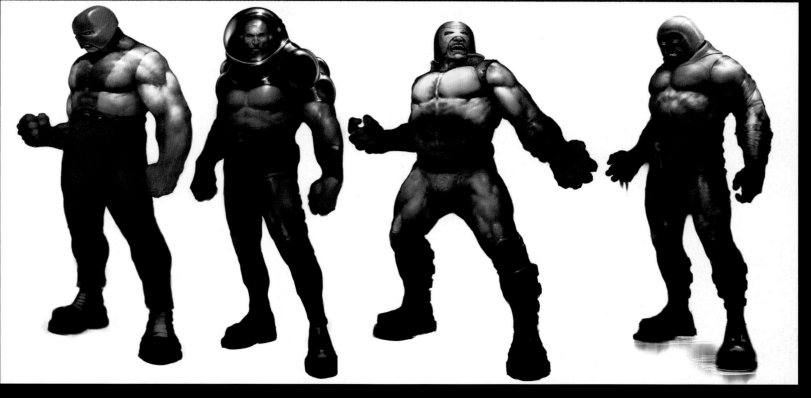

In order to "build" Juggernaut, designers started with drawings (following input from Marvel). Once the actor was in place they started doing three-dimensional views. Finally a life cast was made for prosthetics and—after four hours in the makeup chair—everything fit like a glove.

—Jayne Dancose, Special Effects

Juggernaut concept illustrations by Carlos Huante for Spectral Motion Inc.

X3.125

Option-A

Option-B

Option-C

Option-D

Option-E

Concept illustrations for Juggernaut's helmet by Constantine Sekeris for Spectral Motion Inc.

Vinnie Jones doesn't need the Juggernaut outfit to look scary and powerful. He's like a train coming at you two hundred miles an hour without it. But seeing him in the muscle suit, enhancing what he has already, makes him scarier. He's incredibly famous for being strong, violent, and powerful, yet he brings a certain flavor to the role. It was a fun thing for him to do because he gets to do what he does—destroy everything.

—Avi Arad, Producer

ABOVE: Full body illustration of Juggernaut by Constantine Sekeris for Spectral Motion Inc.
RIGHT: Juggernaut/Cain Marko portrayed by former British soccer star Vinnie Jones

Concept drawings of the aftermath at the Jean Grey house by, from top to bottom, Paolo Venturi, James Clyne, and Daren Dochterman. BELOW: Wolverine (Hugh Jackman) and Storm (Halle Berry) confront Juggernaut outside the Jean Grey house. OPPOSITE: Storyboards by Brent Boates.

ext. jean grey house..

HOUSE HOVERS AND....

...FALLS

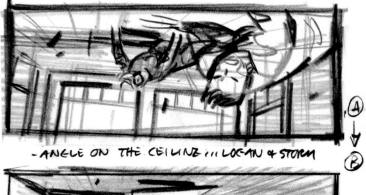

-ANGLE ON THE CEILING ... LOGAN & STORM

... ARE BLOWN OUT THE WINDOW...

-EXT HOUSE - LOGAN & STORM ARE BLOWN OUT THE WINDOW...

-LOGAN & STORM ON THE STREET....

X3.131

132.X3

ABOVE and BELOW: Concept illustrations of Magneto's underground lair by Milena Zdravkovic. LEFT: Ian McKellen on the hideout set.

I love Magneto because I created a really original character. And while he was the foe of the good guys—not really that bad— I wanted it to be as though you could almost understand and sympathize with him, because he and Professor X are really opposite sides of the same coin.

—Stan Lee

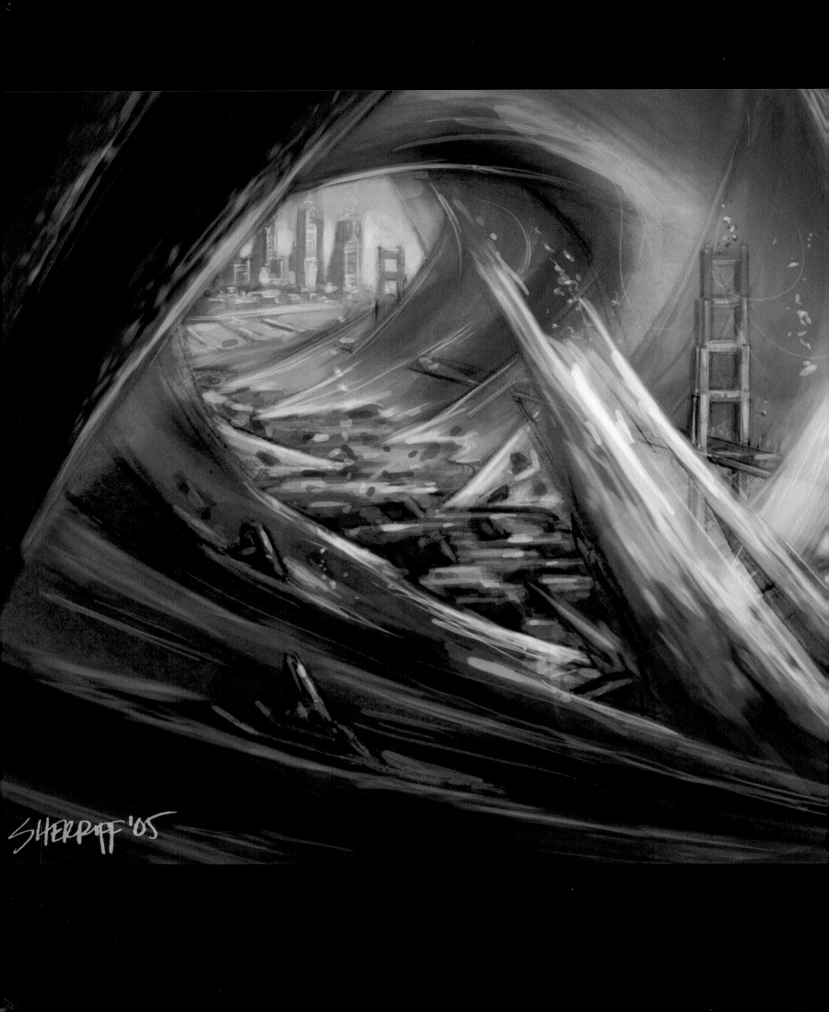

X-Men: The Last Stand

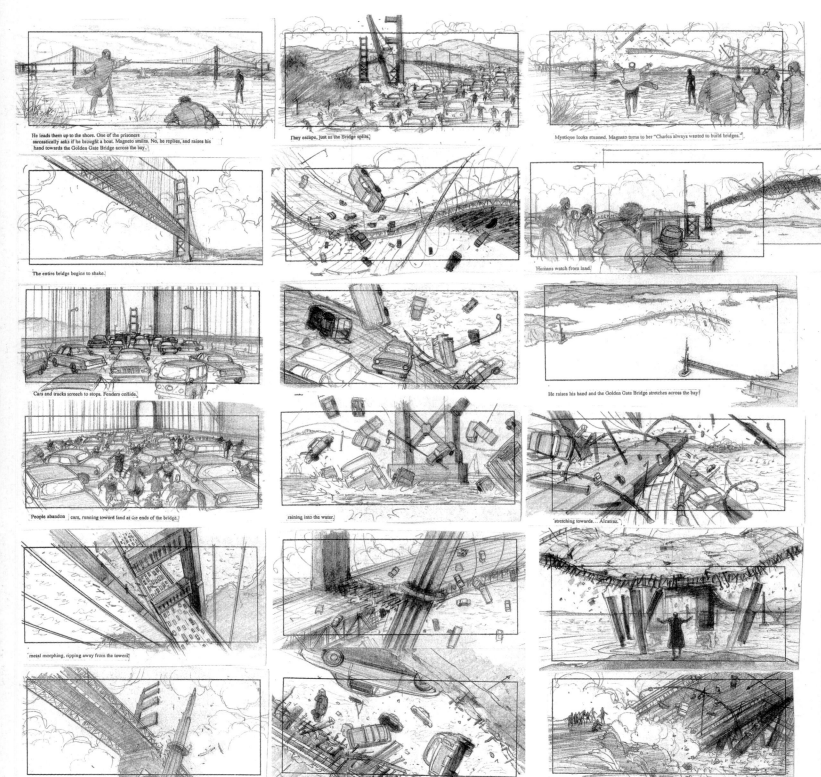

He leads them up to the shore. One of the prisoners sarcastically asks if he brought a boat. Magneto smiles. No, he replies, and raises his hand towards the Golden Gate Bridge across the bay.

They escape, just as the Bridge splits.

Mystique looks stunned. Magneto turns to her "Charles always wanted to build bridges."

The entire bridge begins to shake.

Humans watch from land.

Cars and trucks screech to stops. Fenders collide.

He raises his hand and the Golden Gate Bridge stretches across the bay.

People abandon cars, running toward land at the ends of the bridge.

raining into the water.

stretching towards... Alcatraz.

metal morphing, ripping away from the towers.

Magneto is ripping the Bridge apart.

Clang! The bridge hits the shore of Alcatraz. "Exodus" quotes Magneto, and then

Storyboards by Michael A. Jackson.

PREVIOUS SPREAD: Destruction of San Francisco Bay concept illustration by Dean Sherriff. ABOVE RIGHT: Paolo Venturi's concept illustration of the Golden Gate Bridge landing on Alcatraz. CENTER RIGHT: Digital effect of the Golden Gate Bridge under Magneto's control. BELOW RIGHT: Concept drawing by James Clyne of Magneto's assault on Alcatraz. BELOW: The Brotherhood arrives on Alcatraz.

There are a lot of spectacular scenes in the movie but one is going to be talked about—the Golden Gate Bridge scene. It's magnificent: cables popping, stones falling, metal bending, cars sliding, people running, and then the Brotherhood march over to Alcatraz where the X-Men greet and fight them. What we've learned, though, is that the human element, their relationships, are really the heart and soul of these movies. It's not about saving a nameless, faceless crowd. It's about saving Rogue, Storm, and Logan. Still, it is a big spectacular scene—one with a lot of dramatic tension.

—Lauren Shuler Donner, Producer

138.X3

The palette of X-3 is so much bigger than it was in the other X-Movies, particularly in the arena of action. Magneto says, "The war has begun," and finally we get to bring that large-scale battle to the screen. The X-Men use their powers as a team to battle the Brotherhood with action and effects at a level that's unprecedented.

—David Gorder, Associate Producer

ABOVE: Concept illustration of the Mutant battle for Alcatraz by Warren Flanagan.

X3.139

Storyboard panels of the mutant battle by Collin Grant.

X3.141

142.X3

Simon Crane, our second unit director, has been up here hurling cars with cranes and big hydraulic machines, launching cars—pressurized gas exploding them—and we'll be just interacting all the effects with that. The end of the film is pretty spectacular.

—John Bruno,
VFX Supervisor

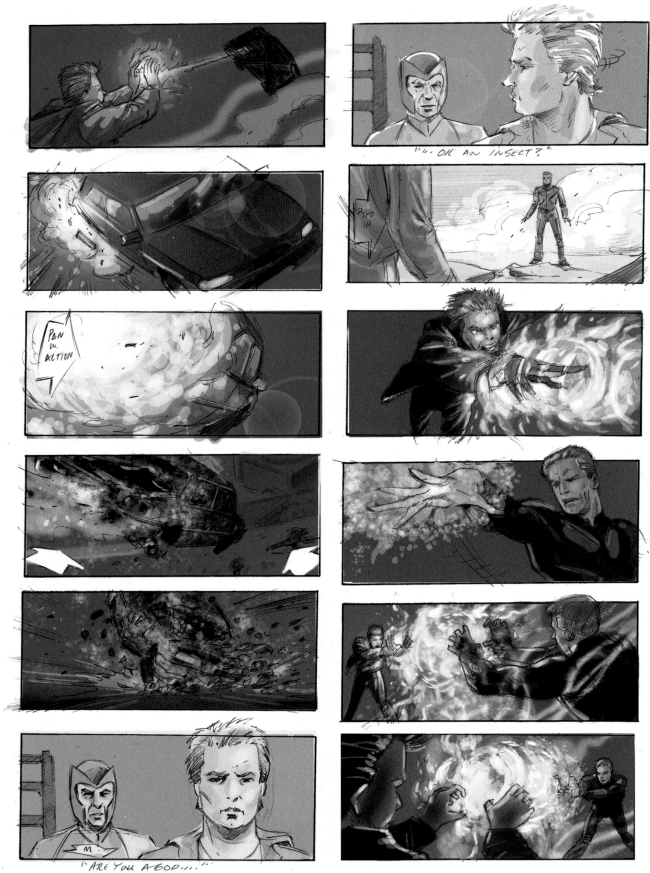

Storyboards by Adrien Van Viersen.

146.X3

X-Men: The Last Stand

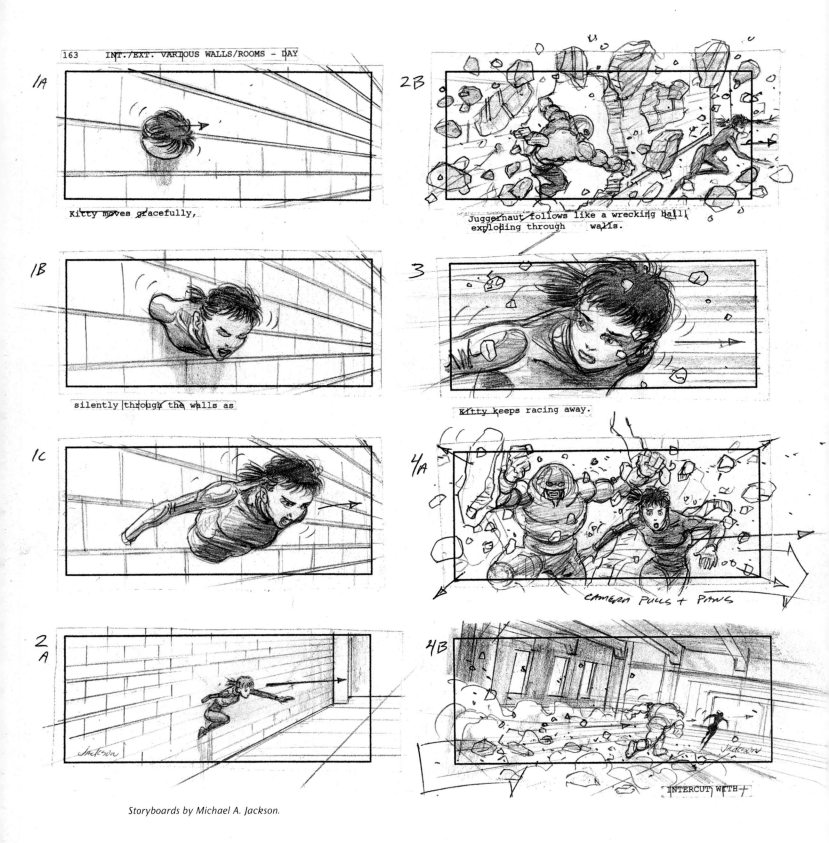

Storyboards by Michael A. Jackson.

148.X3

Juggie's like a mercenary. He's incredibly strong, definitely unstoppable, just raw strength and lives for battles. But he's a cool dude.

—Vinnie Jones, "Juggernaut"

152.X3

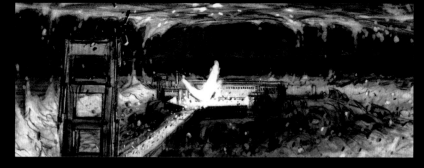

In X-Men 1 there are inklings that something is wrong with Jean. In X2 she's having headaches and her fate is uncertain. In X3 Jean Grey is back and at the heart of the movie, but she is reborn as Dark Phoenix, a woman with powers so vast that they literally drive her mad.

—Zak Penn, Co-Screenwriter

LEFT and BELOW: Dean Sherriff's concept illustrations of the Golden Gate Bridge sequence. TOP RIGHT: Storyboard panel of Dark Phoenix's arrival to Alcatraz by Brent Boates. RIGHT: Two digital schematics continue the same scene.

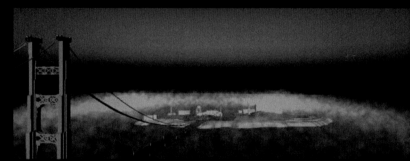

154.X3

Concept illustration of the destruction of Dark Phoenix by Warren Flanagan.

X3.155

156.X3

Wolverine's struggle is on many levels. He's not exactly sure who he is—he literally can't remember. So he's on his own, he relies on himself in every way. But the other side of Wolverine is his incredible heart and his strong connection to very few people. Jean Grey, someone he loves deeply, is one of them. And in X3 he has to make a wrenching choice about her— the toughest choice he will ever make. It's incredibly tragic.

—Hugh Jackman, "Wolverine"

RIGHT: Concept drawing of Wolverine's final confrontation with Dark Phoenix by Paolo Venturi.

She rises from the ashes— coming out of a lake—part Jean Grey and part instinctual creature with very little control over her extreme powers, which now exceed even those of her mentor, Xavier. Everything that he's taught her has gone out the window. She's more powerful than anybody.

—Famke Janssen, "Jean Grey"